INSIGHT

COSTA BRAVA

Compact Guide: Costa Brava is the ideal quick-reference guide to one of Spain's most popular destinations. It tells you everything you need to know about the region's attractions, from the bustle of Barcelona to the peace of the Pyrennees, from remote Romanesque monasteries to masterpieces of modern art, and from enchanting coves to the liveliest resorts.

This is one of 133 Compact Guides, combining the interests and enthusiasms of two of the world's best-known information providers: Insight Guides, whose innovative titles have set the standard for visual travel guides since 1970, and Discovery Channel, the world's premier source of nonfiction television programming.

Discovery
CHANNEL

APA PUBLICATIONS
Part of the Langenscheidt Publishing Group

Star Attractions

An instant reference to some of Costa Brava's most popular tourist attractions to help you on your way.

Barcelona p14

Tarragona p27

Girona p31

Portbou p35

Figueres p38

Corniche to Tossa p46

Lloret de Mar p47

Sitges p49

Wine region p90

Val d'Aran p65

Lleida p68

Costa Brava

The Costa Brava – Queen of Catalonia

Many people tend to equate the northeast of Spain with the Costa Brava, the northern section of coast that starts at the Spanish border. The fact that Costa Brava has almost become synonymous with a Spanish seaside holiday is not surprising: people have been coming here for decades, enticed by the wonderful mixture of golden sand and pine-backed bays, sheer cliffs and secret coves. But the Costa Brava forms only a part of a much larger region whose coast extends south, past the Costa del Maresme, beyond Barcelona and on to the flat golden beaches of the Costa Daurada, or 'Gold Coast', for a total distance of some 580km (360 miles).

Estartit on the Costa Brava

Catalonia is a region which, despite occupying only around one sixteenth of the entire Spanish land mass, has a great deal to offer. The capital, Barcelona, has become an international household name ever since it hosted the 1992 Olympics; Antoni Gaudí's masterpiece, the Sagrada Família, is the symbol of the city, and the *Rambla*, the animated street at the centre of Barcelona, epitomises its multicultural existence.

Plaça de Catalunya, heart of Barcelona

5

But the real mysteries of this 1,000-year-old autonomous region are hidden further inland. Catalonia boasts such attractive towns as Girona, Tarragona and Lleida, for instance, where secular rulers assured themselves of clerical support by building magnificent Gothic cathedrals. In the fertile plains or in the mountains, little towns and villages radiate rural tranquillity. Numerous Romanesque churches and monasteries dotted right across the region recall Catalonia's heyday between the 12th and 14th centuries when it was ruled by the counts of Barcelona and the kings of Aragón, and even controlled whole countries such as Sicily or Sardinia.

Visitors wishing to get away from it all can take a trip into the beautiful Pyrenees, where hiking is still a real adventure and strangers are greeted with genuine curiosity and interest. The hills and valleys, and the high mountain air, can be an exhilarating experience. Catalonia and the Costa Brava have much more to offer their visitors than just sun, sand and sea.

Hostalets d'En Bas, in Girona's rural heartland

Position and Landscape

Catalonia covers an area of 31,930sq km (12,320sq miles). It extends from the Pyrenees in the north to the Ebre Valley in the southwest, and roughly 250km inland from the Mediterranean coast as far as the hilly province of Aragón. The impressive ramparts of the Pyrenees (highest peak: Pico de Aneto, 3,404m/11,168ft) mark the border with France to the north; the rivers Segre and Noguera

flow from here into the Riu Ebre. Three major mountain ranges extend north-south across the region: Montseny (1,712m/5,616ft), Montserrat (1,236m/4,055ft) and the Serra de Prades (1,201m/3,940ft). The rivers from this region, such as the Riu Ter and the Riu Llobregat, flow straight into the sea.

The interior of Catalonia is very fertile, thanks to the many rivers and their subsidiary canals. Agriculture is everywhere in evidence: olives, almonds, fruit and vegetables, wine cultivation and dairy farming are all common sights. Catalonia's wines are often a real discovery: the region lies on the same latitude as Tuscany, and its potent reds, high-quality whites and luscious dessert wines are delicious, to say nothing of its famous *cava* sparkling wine (*see page 90*).

Vineyard in Cava country

Flora and fauna

Typical plants along the coast are agaves, pine-trees, fig-cacti and various types of palm-tree which were only introduced during the 19th century. The central mountain ranges still have several thick forests of chestnut, oak and pine, though even the most remote mountain regions bear evidence of deforestation – which has been going on ever since the Middle Ages when wood was needed to build ships. Forest fires and pollution have also left their mark. In spring and autumn the tiny mountain streams become raging torrents and tear much of the rootless soil along with them, often washing away whole slopes – and sections of beach, too, when they reach the sea.

Like the rest of Europe, Catalonia has very few large animals still living wild; the odd chamois, eagle or bear can only be found high up in the mountains. These days environmental groups are trying to change things, however, and several areas have already been saved from complete ecological ruin.

Glass-bottomed boat in Lloret

The Costa Brava

In today's tourist catalogues the name Costa Brava is used to describe the 214km (132 miles) of Catalonian coast between Portbou in the north and Blanes in the south, with its white sandy beaches, blue sky and tourist centres. When the journalist Ferrán Agulló coined the term at the end of the 19th century he may have had something rather different in mind.

The word *bravo* has several meanings: its first meaning, 'impassable' or 'elemental', very aptly describes the short stretch of coast around Cadaqués and between Sant Feliu de Guíxols and Tossa de Mar. Agulló was standing up at the Ermita Sant Elm and looking down at the bizarre rock formations. He was also aware of just how 'wild' the sea can be here (the second meaning of the word

Promenade party, Barcelona

bravo), especially when it gets whipped up by the cold northern wind known as the *tramuntana*; fishing boats and even larger vessels get flung on to the rocks. The slightly warmer wind known as the *garbí* shouldn't be underestimated either: it doesn't create a lot of waves, but it still keeps everything floating pinned to the shore. Agulló may also have been thinking of the people along this stretch of coast, who bravely (the third meaning of the word *bravo*) venture out in their fishing boats day after day, hoping for calm seas.

Climate and when to go

For a relatively small area, Catalonia has a climate as varied as its geography. The average summer temperature along the coast is 26°C/79°F (with a night-time temperature between June and September of 19°C/66°F), with around 200 days' sunshine annually, though the northern part of the Costa Brava can get very windy (*see above*). Water temperatures fluctuate between 14°C in December and 24°C (57–75°F) in August. Rain is rare, usually falling from March to May and from mid-September to mid-November. Inland, the Catalonian climate is hot and dry during the summer, but nearer the Pyrenees precipitation tends to be higher and temperatures are lower.

Costa Brava cove

Wildlife walk, Aiguamolls

The best time for a seaside holiday is between June and September. Because of the summer heat, spring and autumn may be the preferred seasons for those wishing to engage in serious sight-seeing or long-distance walking. In the high Pyrenees the summer months are also ideal.

The Catalans – language and culture

Catalonia has a population of almost 6 million, and Catalans make up around 60 percent of it. The rest are mainly immigrants who arrived in the region from Southern Spain in the 1960s and also more recent immigration, much from Latin America. Catalonia today has the highest population density of any Spanish region.

Politically, most Catalans feel they belong more to Europe than to Spain. *Europa no comença als Pirineus*, 'Europe doesn't begin at the Pyrenees,' as they say. The Catalans are rather more European in habits and outlook than their other Spanish compatriots, and have a reputation for hard work and shrewdness in business. The decision to allow Barcelona to host the Olympics in 1992 was a great boost to Catalan national pride.

The Catalans' language is known as *català* (Catalan). Written evidence of this independent, Latin-derived language dates from as early as the 12th century. It has nothing in common with Castilian (present-day Spanish); Catalan is related instead to the Provençal language of Southern France and is also spoken on the Balearic Islands, around Valencia, and even in parts of Sardinia. Thus, the words may look familiar, but definitely come from a language which belongs on its own. Beaches are neither *plages* nor *playas*, but *platjas*, good day is *bon dia,* please is *si us plau*, and welcome is neither *bienvenu* nor *bienvenidos*, but *benvinguts*.

The 18th-century Spanish kings and General Franco tried to suppress the use of Catalan, but without success. Since the return of democracy in 1975, and with it some degree of autonomy for Catalonia, Catalan has blossomed. Today it has achieved the status of an official language; lessons in schools and universities in Catalonia take place in Catalan and Castilian, and official proclamations are also published in the two languages. Most place names have now been 'catalanised' as well.

With this blossoming has come a renewed, overt pride; a remembrance, for example, that Catalonia was one of the great seafaring nations, that it has been and often still is a leader in the arts and in industry, that its food and wine are unparalleled… A number of old local traditions are being revived these days as well. Catalans don't dance flamenco, for instance: young and old alike dance the *sardana*, an ancient popular dance (*see page 86*). They don't particularly enjoy bullfights, either, preferring instead the delights of FC Barcelona (football).

8

A nation of seafarers…
…and fanatical football fans

Politics and Administration

Since 1979 Catalonia has been an autonomous region, forming part of the Spanish constitutional monarchy which has existed since the death of General Franco in 1975. The fundamentals for autonomy were laid down in the 'autonomy statute' of 1979, which gave competence to the Catalan government, or *generalitat*. Based in Barcelona (Plaça de Sant Jaume, Barri Gòtic), the latter regards itself as the direct descendant of the *Corts Generals*, first formed in the year 1359. The government consists of a unicameral, 135-member parliament and an executive council headed by a president. Jordi Pujol of the moderate CDC party *(Convergència Democràtica de Catalunya)* has been president since 1980. In co-operation with the *Unió Democràtica de Catalunya*, his party (CIU) is now the strongest in the region. Other important political parties include the *Partit Socialista de Catalunya* (PSC-PSOE) and the three-party-coalition known as *Iniciativa par Catalunya* (IC).

Catalan and Spanish flags

From the administrative point of view, Catalonia is divided into four provinces: Barcelona, Tarragona, Girona and Lleida. These are divided in turn into 41 administrative districts known as *comarques*, created after 1987 according to various regional peculiarities and economic considerations.

The Economy

From the economic point of view, Catalonia has now become the most successful of Spain's regions. Its 6 million inhabitants form just 15 percent of the national population, but are responsible for creating over 20 percent of its gross national product.

9

Industry – and especially the service sector – has taken over from agriculture as the primary source of revenue. Catalonia's most important trading partners are the European Union countries. Its main export partner is Germany, and it receives most imports from France. Catalonian industry is concentrated almost exclusively around Greater Barcelona, where more than half the population lives and works. In the other parts of the region, tourism is the largest source of income. Catalonia is visited annually by around 15 million people, and as a result the tourist infrastructure is excellent.

Down by the port

Historical Highlights

c 700BC The first inhabitants of today's Catalonia to leave traces for recorded history are the Iberians from North Africa. They also settle the region around today's Barcelona.

c 600BC The Greeks reach the coast of Catalonia and found several ports, including Emporion (Empúries).

300BC The Carthaginians reach Catalonia, and the Romans arrive in the area of today's Catalonia in the year 217BC. In 197BC, a peace treaty ends the First Punic War between Rome and Carthage. The Carthaginians withdraw from the region and the Romans found the province of Hispania Citerior, with its capital at Tarraco (today's Tarragona).

200BC–AD200 The region flourishes under the Romans, especially the towns of Tarragona and Barcelona; the latter, known as Julia Augusta Favencia Paterna Barcino, enjoys a long period of economic prosperity.

414 After the collapse of Roman rule, the Visigoths conquer Northern Spain, and in 476 they capture the city of Barcelona which they make the capital of their empire of Gotalonia. It is widely believed that the name Catalonia originated in this way.

587 The Visigothic King Reccared converts to Christianity.

711 Hordes of Moors travel north from Africa across Spain and also spend a brief period in Catalonia. They capture Barcelona in 717.

8th and 9th centuries The Carolingians, led by Louis the Pious, force the Moors to retreat from Catalonia and also take Barcelona. Count Wilfred the Hairy of Barcelona (873–98) eventually takes advantage of the gradual disintegration of the Carolingian Empire to assert his independence, and secures control of several other counties. The dynasty he founds rules in Catalonia until the 15th century.

985, 988 The Moors, led by Almansor ('the Victorious'), conquer Barcelona and inflict great damage. However, the city is rescued in 988 despite lack of assistance from the Franks. Count Borell of Barcelona now completely rejects Frankish suzerainty. 988 is still celebrated as marking the birth of Catalonia.

11th–15th centuries The flowering of Benedictine monasticism and of the Catalan Romanesque style of architecture.

1137 Count Ramón Berenguer IV marries Petronila, Queen of Aragón, and Barcelona becomes its capital. The pact with Aragón turns Catalonia into a mighty maritime power; in the 13th century it occupies large sections of the Mediterranean, including Sardinia and Naples.

1276 Death of Jaume I, the conqueror under whom Catalonia reached the limits of its expansion and among other things, increased its power at sea.

1289 The Corts Catalanes – the representative bodies of the clergy, the secular nobility and the cities of Aragón, Catalonia and Valencia – meet for the first time. They are the first form of parliamentary government anywhere in Europe.

1469 Ferdinand II of Aragón marries Isabella of Castile. With the Moors driven out of the country, Spain is unified and the capital of the resulting absolute monarchy is shifted to Madrid. Catalonia and Barcelona are denied trading rights with the New World, and their economic decline is a foregone conclusion.

1492 The ships of Christopher Columbus set sail from Barcelona to find the New World.

1640 A secessionist revolt, supported by King Louis XIII of France, takes place against the Spanish king Philip IV, and the Spanish troops only finally win back Barcelona in 1652.

1702 During the War of the Spanish Succession, Catalonia declares its support for the archduke Charles of Austria, and suffers dearly as a result. In 1714 Philip V occupies Barcelona, partially razing it to the ground.

1716 Philip V's *Decreto de Nueva Planta* abolishes Catalan law, language and institutions.

1778 Catalonia is allowed to trade with the Americas (previously the monopoly of Seville and Cadiz). Exports of cork and imports of cotton provide the basis of the region's expanding economy.

1808–14 A Catalan uprising against the French results in the so-called Peninsula War. Napoleon invades the country, damaging much of Barcelona and also the Monastery of Montserrat.

1814 onwards Catalonia profits from the Industrial Revolution and becomes the most economically successful region of the country. Spain's first ever steam engine (1833) and railway (1848, between Barcelona and Mataró) are both built in Catalonia.

1859 Revival of Jocs Floral literary festival, marks the beginning of the Catalan cultural reawakening.

mid-19th century onwards The decision is made to raze the citadel erected in Barcelona by Philip V, and construction work begins on the Eixample (New Town). Catalan culture and language experience a rebirth (Renaixença) that finds its reflection in literature, painting and architecture (Modernisme).

1871 Catalonia declares its independence from Spain, but after negotiations still remains part of the Spanish kingdom.

1888 Barcelona's Universal Exhibition, a celebration of Catalan economic and industrial achievement, is held on the area formerly occupied by the citadel. Numerous *Modernisme* buildings appear in the city.

1914 A Catalan provincial government, the Mancomunitat Catalana, is appointed. However, it is unable to hold its own against the 1923 military dictatorship of Primo di Rivera.

1929 Barcelona's second Universal Exhibition is held on Montjuïc.

1932 Under the Second Spanish Republic (1931–9) Catalonia receives its first statute of autonomy, and Francesc Macià becomes the first president. This period of rejoicing doesn't last long, however.

1936 Start of the Spanish Civil War.

1939 On 26 January, troops loyal to Franco march into Barcelona, which is on the Republican side. Lluís Companys, the president of the republic, is executed on Montjuïc. The Catalan culture is suppressed for many years. Workers from other regions of Spain are settled in Barcelona systematically.

1960–75 During the economic miracle of the 1960s and 1970s, Barcelona grows larger and larger. Vast dormitory towns appear. Resistance against the Franco regime is forced underground. The Catholic church is the only body to recognise Catalan as an official language. The 1960s also see the beginning of the Costa Brava package-tour boom.

1977 Two years after Franco's death (1975) a referendum is held, and the constitutional monarchy is introduced. Juan Carlos I becomes the Spanish king, Catalonia receives its second statute of autonomy in 1979, and Catalan is recognised as the official language. After the first free parliamentary elections in 1980, Jordi Pujol becomes president of the autonomous region.

1986 Spain joins the European Community. Barcelona is named host of the XXV Olympic Games. Catalonia and its capital increasingly become a focus of world attention.

1986 onwards Much building activity in and around Barcelona. New streets, offices and hotels appear. A total of £6bn/US$9bn is invested in the modernisation programme.

1992 Barcelona hosts the 1992 Olympics, and refurbishs its road infrastructure (ringroads or *rondas*).

1993 Spain becomes a full member of the European Union.

1996 José María Aznar is elected Prime Minister after the Conservatives win the elections.

1999 Having been gutted by fire in 1994, Barcelona's Gran Teatre del Liceu is reopened.

2002 The Euro replaces the peseta.

2004 Barcelona to host the Cultural 'Forum 2004', with further city and beach development.

Route 1

Barcelona

The capital of the autonomous region of Catalonia likes to think of itself as Spain's gateway to Europe. Of the total of 6 million Catalans, 3 million live in Greater Barcelona, and more than half of them live in the city centre. The economy of the Catalonian capital has meanwhile overtaken that of Madrid, with most of the population working either in industry or in the service sector. Barcelona is one of the most important ports in the Mediterranean; its airport, extended in 1992, is now one of the busiest in Europe. In addition to its architectural attractions, Barcelona has more than 50 museums, 10 theatres, a world-famous university, hundreds of restaurants and bars, and a vast selection of cultural events and festivals all year round.

The most fascinating parts of the city are its Old Town around the Rambla and the Barri Gòtic (Gothic Quarter), but the New Town, or Eixample, with its numerous art nouveau buildings, is also definitely worth a visit. The museums and sports centres up on the hills surrounding the city (Montjuïc, Tibidabo) should not be missed either. Those with enough time on their hands should definitely travel the 50km (31 miles) to the Monastery of Montserrat, the Catalonian national shrine.

14

Gaudí's Casa Batlló
Tibidabo's amusement park

History

The earliest archaeological finds in the area occupied by Barcelona today point to an Iberian settlement (c 1000BC). The Iberians were followed by the Greeks, the Carthaginians and then the Romans. Barcelona was then conquered in turn by the Visigoths and the Moors. It was only after the latter had been driven out by the Franks that some degree of political stability was achieved, and after the autonomous 'county of Barcelona' was announced by Count Borell II in the year 988, the foundations were laid for a state of Catalonia, of which Barcelona became the centre. Thanks to the marriage of Count Berenguer IV of Barcelona to the future queen of Aragón in 1137, Catalonia developed into a major political power in Europe. Catalonian ships sailed as far as Naples and Sardinia.

Barcelona character

From 1469 onwards, however, when the kingdoms of Castile and Aragón were united by marriage, Barcelona's fortunes began to decline. The city was barred from trading with the newly-discovered lands in America, and Madrid as centre of government became increasingly dominant. During the War of the Spanish Succession, Barcelona declared its support for the wrong side, and after the Habsburgs were defeated (1714) the city was occupied by the troops of King Philip V. Catalan was banned from use as an official language, and the economy lay in ruins.

It didn't take Barcelona long to recover from its plight, however: the city became the catalyst for the industrial revolution in Spain and also a centre of artistic development. During the 19th century there was a renaissance of Catalan culture *(Renaixença)* which received international acclaim when the first world fair in Barcelona was held in 1888. The New Town, built from 1860 onwards, was a superb architectural achievement; several exponents of *Modernisme* (Gaudí, Domènech i Montaner, Puig i Cadafalch), the special Catalan version of art nouveau, made their unique contributions (*see page 84*). After the turmoil of World War I, Barcelona hosted a world fair yet again in 1929 – but 10 years later in 1939 the city's days of glory ended abruptly when it was occupied by Franco's troops.

Barcelona suffered under the Fascist regime for a full 36 years, its language and customs suppressed. It was only in 1979 that Catalonia became an 'autonomous region' and Barcelona became its capital. The city freed itself from the constraints of the past surprisingly quickly and was soon back on the international stage, hosting the 25th Olympic Games in 1992. The economy and the construction business are both booming at the moment, not always to the advantage of either the population or the city's centuries-old infrastructure.

Tour 1: The Rambla and the Harbour

One 'must' for any visitor to Barcelona is a stroll along the ★★★ **Rambla**, the 1.2-km (¾-mile) long shopping street in the Old Town. It follows the course of an old riverbed, and extends from Plaça de Catalunya to the harbour.

The Olympic Port

15

Strolling along the Rambla

Canaletes Fountain

The Rambla is busy at almost any time of day or night: newspapers, flowers and even birds and pets are sold at the many stands, and live street theatre performances are common. This is definitely the heart of Barcelona. The upper section of this plane-tree-lined boulevard is called the **Rambla de Canaletes**, named after the drinking fountain at the top of the street where the fans of the FC Barcelona football team always gather after every win. The **Rambla dels Estudis**, so named because it used to be popular with students from the old university nearby, has

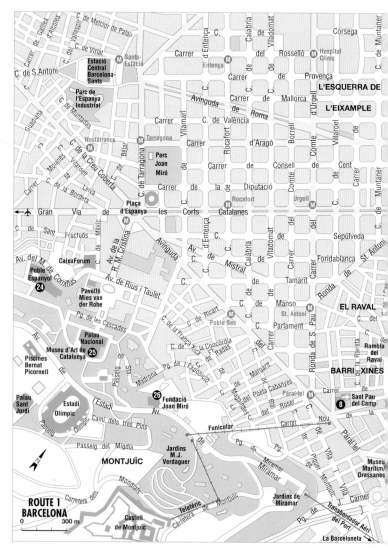

the **Teatre Poliorama** ❶ on its right-hand side; it was built in 1883 by Domènech i Estapa. The Carrer Pintor Fortuny leads down westwards into the older and rather downtrodden area of the city known as El Raval, which has been given a cultural boost with the startlingly-modern **Musée d'Art Contemporani (MACBA)** ❷, designed by Richard Meyer and a venue for sculpture and installation art, (Monday to Friday 11am–8pm, Saturday 10am–8pm, Sunday 10am–3pm). Beside it, the old Casa de la Caritat is now the CCCB cultural centre with temporary exhibitions.

Teatre Poliorama

17

The old Jesuit church of **Mare Déu Betlem** ❸, built between 1687 and 1729 can be seen on the corner of the Carrer del Carme. On the opposite side of the Rambla dels Estudis, on the corner of the Carrer Portaferrissa, is the **Palau Moja** ❹, an 18th-century palazzo with a fine inner courtyard and also a bookstore with some fascinating publications on Catalonia. This is where the **Rambla de Sant Josep** begins, the two highlights of which are the **Palau de la Virreina** ❺ (the 'Vicereine's Palace', built between 1772 and 1778 by Marquès de Castellbell) and the ★★ **Mercat de Sant Josep** ❻. This market, also known as *la boqueria* (literally: 'the gullet'), contains just about every gourmet speciality known to man: fresh fruit and vegetables, seafood, etc. Notice the two famous restaurants here, the Pinotxo and the Gardunya. The cast iron portal with its stained glass decorations dates from 1835.

On the other side of the Plaça Sant Agustí, with its 18th-century church, the high walls of the 11th-century **Antic Hospital de la Santa Creu** ❼ enclose two idyllic interior courtyards. Today the hospital buildings house the university's medical faculty and central library. Exhibitions are held in the hospital chapel.

The large mosaic by Joan Miró and the Casa Bruno Quadras with its umbrella facade point the way down the narrow Carrer Cardenal Casañas. A few yards further on it opens out into the delightfully tranquil ★★ **Plaça del Pi**, with the Gothic church of the same name. The café in this leafy square is a popular meeting place and buskers often perform on account of the excellent acoustics.

The **Rambla dels Caputxins**, named after a Capuchin monastery that formerly stood on the site, has a turn-off to the right called the Carrer Sant Pau. Walk down it for about 10 minutes to reach the small but magnificent Romanesque church of ★ **Sant Pau del Camp** ❽. The

Plaça del Pi

Fruit stall in the boqueria

entrance portal dates from 1120, and there is a delightful ★ cloister adjoining the church to the south. When the church was built in around the year 1000 it stood outside the city walls, 'in the fields' – hence the name.

At the junction of the Rambla and the Carrer Sant Pau stands Barcelona's world-famous opera house, the **Gran Teatre del Liceu** . Built in 1845 and seating over 5,000 people, the opera house had to be completely rebuilt following a disastrous fire in 1994. It was reopened in October 1999 to the strains of Puccini's *Turandot*, the same work that was being performed when the fire broke out.

The most unusual building in the Carrer Nou de la Rambla is an early work by Antoni Gaudí: the ★ **Palau Güell** ❿ (Monday to Saturday 10am– 6.15pm in summer, 10am–4.30pm in winter). The master of *Modernisme* created this interesting mixture of Moorish and Gothic elements in 1888 for his patron, Count Güell, on a plot of land measuring just 18m (60ft) by 12m (39ft). Opposite the Carrer Nou de la Rambla, the short Carrer Colom points the way to the ★ **Plaça Reial**. This magnificent square, laid out in 1848, with its arcades, cafés and restaurants, is a meeting-point for visitors from all over the world. Street musicians and jugglers can often be seen performing here.

Plaça Reial

19

Along the **Rambla de Santa Mónica**, the main attractions apart from the ★ **Museu de Cera** (a wax museum with models of the famous) are clairvoyants, portrait painters and readers of tea-leaves and coffee-grounds. Each weekend a large craft fair is also held here.

At the end of the pedestrian precinct and visible from afar is the **Monument a Colom** ⓫, erected in 1888 in memory of Christopher Columbus; there is a fine view of the section of the city that faces the sea from its observation platform. The different types of ships used by Barcelona's mariners and their various destinations can be studied in the ★ **Museu Marítim** (daily 10am–7pm, except Tuesday and Friday 10am–11pm), which is housed in the halls of the 13th-century royal shipyards nearby. Or why not set sail yourself – the little boats known as *golondrinas* (literally: 'swallows') on the modern promenade of Moll de la Fusta do round trips of the harbour.

Monument a Colom

Museu Marítim in the old royal shipyards

Outside the harbour office a wooden bridge known as the Rambla del Mar leads to the **Maremagnum** superstore complex which also contains exhibition rooms, restaurants, an Imax cinema, and Europe's largest aquarium. North of here is the harbour quarter of Port Vell with its renovated **Palau de Mar**, now a hands-on museum of Catalan history (daily 10am–7pm, except Wednesday 10am–8pm and Sunday 10am–2.30pm, closed Monday), yacht harbour and promenade; round off this tour with a visit to one of the excellent seafood restaurants in the Barceloneta fishing quarter.

Inside the Casa de la Ciutat

Plaça de Sant Felip Neri

Jaume I outside the Town Hall

Tour 2: Barri Gòtic

Every traveller to Barcelona should allow themselves at least half a day to explore the city's ★★ **Gothic Quarter** *(*Barri Gòtic). It was here, on the small rise known as Mons Taber (12m/39ft), that the city was first settled, and it is here that traces of Roman and all subsequent cultures are regularly found.

The Barri Gòtic is like the centre of a tree-trunk, around which the other sections of the city have grown like rings. The two Roman watchtowers of the Portal de Bisbe look very forbidding; pass between them to gain access to the historic Barri Gòtic from the Plaça Nova. Go past the Palau Episcopal, and carry on as far as the monument (1918) to those who fell during the Napoleonic Wars, situated at the centre of the little square of Garriga i Bachs. From here the tranquil ★ **Plaça de Sant Felip Neri** is just a few steps away. The church and also the adjoining building, which houses a **shoe museum** ⓫, both date from the 17th century. Public executions were carried out here during the Civil War (note the marks on the walls made by the rifle bullets).

The northwestern side of the ★ **Plaça de Sant Jaume** is dominated by the **Palau de la Generalitat de Catalunya** ⓭, the seat of government in Catalonia, with its attractive 15th-century ★ inner courtyards and state rooms. Opposite, hardly less imposing, is the **Casa de la Ciutat** ⓮, the Town Hall, which was built in the 19th century. There are several magnificent rooms behind this facade, too, but like the ones in the government building they can only be inspected with prior permission from the information office in the Town Hall.

The narrow Carrer Paradis leads from the northern end of the square. It's hard to imagine that the small door of house No 10 (Centre Excursionista de Catalunya) leads on to the remains of a **Temple of Augustus**  dating from around 100BC.

Cross over now to the impressive medieval square known as the ★★ **Plaça del Rei**. The Catalan and Spanish kings all strode up the steps here leading to the **Palau Reial Major** ⓰, the former royal palace. The building is most famous for its enormous ★ throne room, the Saló del Tinell (built 1356–70), the atrium of which provides access to the 14th-century chapel of Santa Agata and also the rooms housing the ★ **Museu d'Història de la Ciutat** ⓱ (Tuesday to Saturday 10am–8pm in summer, Sunday 10am–3pm). This municipal museum has a fascinating collection of excavated Roman remains in its basement floor; later ages are documented on the upper floors.

Throne room in the palace

The Carrer dels Comtes, beside the cathedral, contains the 16th-century ★ **Palau de Lloctinent** ⓲, and the ★ **Museu Frederic Marès** ⓳. This sculpture museum, founded by the sculptor Marès in 1940, contains an excellent collection of sacred and profane works and also an entertaining 'Museu Sentimental' on the third floor.

Marès Museum sculpture

At the end of the street the Pla de la Seu, the square in front of Barcelona Cathedral, comes into view. At its southwest corner is the **Casa de l'Ardiaca** ⓴; this Late-Gothic building, formerly home to the archdeacon, today houses the city archives and has a magnificent inner courtyard with a Gothic fountain.

Dominating the entire square is the ★ **Cathedral** *(La Seu)*. Earlier Roman-Visigothic structures were incorporated into this building, which was constructed between 1298 and 1448; the facade, however, with its mighty dome, dates from the end of the 19th century. The stunning interior of the three-aisled cathedral, consecrated to Santa Eulalia, contains no less than 29 chapels, the most famous of which is probably the Cappella del Santíssim just to the right of the main portal. It contains a crucifix blackened with rust said to have been worn by the commander of the Christian forces at the Battle of Lepanto in 1571. The Spanish-Gothic-style choir has some fine carving, and in the crypt beneath the main altar, in a white marble sarcophagus (1327), lie the remains of the 13-year-old martyr Santa Eulalia, who died in AD304.

The Cathedral

On the west side of the cathedral, the Porta de Sant Sever leads to the ★ cloister. The various tombs of Barcelona's wealthier citizens are guarded here by a pack of geese, who traditionally live next to the fountain at the centre. The small **Cathedral Museum** (Monday to Friday 10am–1pm and 4–6.30pm, weekends 10am–1pm) on the west side contains several 15th-century religious paintings and sculptures.

Santa Maria del Mar

Pablo Picasso

Tour 3: Parc de la Ciutadella – Olympic Harbour

A three-hour stroll across to Barcelona's leafy ★ **Ciutadella Park** and to the **Olympic Harbour** with its beaches is an excellent way of unwinding from all the busy traffic. The Parc de la Ciutadella was built on the site of the former citadel, razed to the ground during the 19th century, and it contains the city zoo as well as several buildings and sculptures erected here for the world fair in 1888, including the **Museu d'Art Modern** ㉑ (Tuesday to Saturday 10am–7pm, Sunday 10am–2.30pm). From the park it's just a few minutes' walk to the La Ribera section of the city, which contains not only one of the finest Gothic churches in Barcelona, ★ **Santa Maria del Mar** ㉒ (it took just 50 years to build, from 1329 to 1378, which explains its astonishing stylistic unity), but also the world-famous ★★ **Museu Picasso** ㉓ (Carrer Montcada 15–19, Tuesday to Saturday and on holidays 10am–8pm, Sunday 10am–3pm). A collection of over 3,600 works by Picasso, who studied in Barcelona during his youth, is housed here in the rooms of 13th- and 15th-century palazzi.

To the east of the Parc de la Ciutadella lies the Olympic Harbour which, with numerous restaurants and maritime atmosphere. It's also a great place to relax: there's a choice of six brand-new municipal beaches. They're clean, and so is the water apparently. More beach is being developed currently with the Forum 2004.

Tour 4: Montjuïc

The 213-m (698-ft) high hill of Montjuïc, southwest of the city and topped by a castle, has great views and a whole series of sights in store for visitors to Barcelona. Many of the buildings date from the 1929 World Exhibition, and are of great architectural interest. One of these is the

View from the castle on Montjuïc

★ **Mies van der Rohe Pavilion**, a classic of modernist architecture inside and out, or the ★★ **Poble Espanyol**
('Spanish Village', Monday to Saturday 9am–2pm, Sunday 9am–midnight), a fascinating collection of typical buildings from all over Spain, plus several good craft shops and specialist restaurants. Right at the top of the Montjuïc are several important ★ structures dating from the 1992 Olympic Games: the Olympic Stadium (the facade dates from 1929, the rest is state-of-the-art construction technology), the Palau Sant Jordi (seating capacity 17,000) and the Bernat Picornell swimming stadium.

Mies van der Rohe Pavilion

The main attraction up on the Montjuïc, however, are its art museums: the ★★★ **Museu d'Art de Catalunya** (Tuesday to Saturday 10am–7pm, Sunday 10am–2.30pm) and the ★★ **Fundació Joan Miró** (Tuesday to Saturday 10am–8pm, Thursday 10am–9.30pm, Sunday 10am–2.30pm). The former is world-famous for its collection of Romanesque frescoes and paintings – and the Gothic department is excellent, too. The Fundació Joan Miró is devoted to works by the famous Catalan painter (1893–1983), but also puts on exhibitions of work by other contemporary artists. The patio café here is a good place to stop for a snack. The more recent Caixa forum arts complex in an old textile factory has exhibitions and concerts (Tuesday to Sunday 10am–8pm).

23

An entertaining way of rounding off any visit to Montjuïc is to take a trip on the ★ Transbordador Aéri cablecar (departures on the east side of the hill in the Jardins de Miramar, daily noon–8pm) out across the broad harbour basin and back down to the fishing quarter of Barceloneta.

Tour 5: Monuments of Modernisme

A walk along the ★ **Passeig de Gràcia** is a walk into the world of *Modernisme*. More and more art nouveau buildings keep coming into view along the street, each more fascinating than the next. One very impressive group of buildings, the so-called ★★ **Mançana de la Discórdia**
('Block of Discord') is on the corner of Carrer Consell de Cent and Aragó. A series of works by the 'big three' of *Modernisme* can be admired here: Domènech i Montaner designed house No 35, Puig i Cadafalch No 41, and Gaudí No 43 (★★ Casa Battló). After a short detour to the **Fundació Antoni Tàpies** (Carrer Aragó 255, Tuesday to Sunday, 10am–8pm), a museum devoted to works by the abstract painter and housed in an art nouveau building, the ★ **Casa Milà** (Passeig de Gràcia 92, daily 10am–8pm, guided tours in English Monday to Friday 6pm) comes into view. This enormous tenement building designed by Gaudí is still arousing controversy even today.

Casa Lleo Morera at No 35
Casa Milà at No 92

Sagrada Família: Nativity Facade

New sculpture and Gaudí spire

From here it's around 20 minutes' walk down the Carrer Mallorca to the most famous sight in Barcelona, the church of the ★★★ **Sagrada Família** ㉚ (Monday to Sunday 9am–8pm, in winter 9am–6pm). Antoni Gaudí spent over 20 years of his life working on it, but never lived to see its completion. When he died in 1926 only a small part of the eastern facade with the 105-m (344-ft) high tower of St Barnabas (lift to the top, stunning view) had been completed. Gaudí's plans for the building (creating room in the basilica for 15,000 pilgrims, and adding a tower 170m/550ft high) were realised after his death, though construction work was repeatedly brought to a halt, either because of lack of funds or because of artistic controversy.

Several citizens of Barcelona have called for work on the project to be stopped, in order to preserve the purity of Gaudí's original work. Although still incomplete, the building is very impressive indeed. A small museum beneath the basilica contains models and architectural sketches that provide an insight into the history of this 'Temple of the Holy Family'.

Excursions from Barcelona

1. Tibidabo–San Cugat de Vallès

Tibidabo (532m/1,745ft) can be reached either by car along the Carrer de Balmes and then the Avinguda del Tibidabo (12km/7½ miles), or by FCG railway or the *Tibibús* from the Plaça de Catalunya to Tibidabo station. From here, step into the only tram still in existence in Barcelona, the *Tramvia Blau* (daily in summer, otherwise Saturday, Sunday and public holidays only), which takes passengers to

the starting-point of the funicular to the top where there is a fantastic ★ **view** of the host of white houses down in the city, with the blue sea behind, and on smog-free days it's sometimes possible to see as far as Mallorca.

The summit's not exactly the most peaceful of places, however: the **Parc d'Attraccions** ensures that the air's almost permanently filled with the sound of dozens of carousels and other fairground attractions. Nevertheless, despite the relatively high price of admission, it's a good place to take the children. There's also a **Gaming Machine Museum** (winter: Saturday, Sunday and public holidays noon–6pm; summer: Thursday to Sunday noon–10pm) some of the exhibits date from the 19th century, and many can still be operated.

Parc d'Attraccions

Admission to the rather kitschy church of El Sagrat Cor de Jesus (only completed in 1952) is free; the bronze statue of Jesus at the top, a popular backdrop for wedding photos, is 67m (220ft) high.

Those travelling by car can drive on westwards to the hilly landscape of the Sierra de Collserola. It's not far from here to **San Cugat de Vallés** (pop. 30,000), a town that can also be reached from Barcelona's Plaça de Catalunya by FCG railway. Its centre contains several well-preserved art nouveau structures such as the Casa Lluch, built in 1906. The monastery, however, is still the town's main attraction. Originally a Benedictine monastery, it received its first official mention in 897, and it probably grew up above the foundations of the Roman settlement where the bishop Cucuphas was executed in the year 304 during the reign of Diocletian – hence the town's name, San Cugat. The 145 artistically carved capitals by Master Catell (1190) in the Romanesque cloister are particularly fine; beneath them are tombs dating from the 9th century. The monastery church (14th century) contains a valuable altar with a painting by Pere Serra (1375), and also the 14th-century tomb of Abbot Otó.

San Cugat de Vallés

25

2. The Monastery of Montserrat

Early morning is the best time to leave Barcelona by car for this trip, because that allows time to inspect the monastery before the tourist crush begins. Take the A2 and then NII in the direction of Igualada.

A few kilometres outside Olesa de Montserrat, the valley station for the cableway leading up to the Monastery of Montserrat comes into view on the left. Motorists can continue as far as Monistrol. This sleepy little village, repeatedly bothered by the masses of people visiting the monastery, extends along a winding mountain road (8km/5 miles) leading up to the monastery itself. The numerous car parks up here are often completely full, by the way.

The jagged peaks of Montserrat

The ★ **Monastery of Montserrat** (daily 8am–8pm) is situated among the rocky peaks of the ★★ **Serra de Montserrat**; the name literally means 'sawn mountain'. Erosion through the ages has given the peaks – the highest of which is the Turó de Sant Jeroni (1,235m/4,050ft) – their characteristic jagged look. Most of the monastery buildings are recent, because important sections were destroyed and burnt by Napoleonic troops in 1808. The only parts that escaped destruction were the portal of the Romanesque church and sections of the Gothic cloister.

Pilgrims take a rest

This Benedictine monastery was founded in AD880 in honour of a wonder-working statue of the Virgin, which according to legend was discovered in one of the numerous caves nearby. Over the centuries, Montserrat grew into an important place of pilgrimage, and today it is the religious centre of Catalonia. Eighty monks work here, looking after the visitors and running the hotel, the museum, and a massive library with 200,000 books.

The Plaça de Santa Maria, an enormous *parvis* with an impressive view of the nearby sandstone cliffs (Peñascos), is an ideal motif for photographers. Other sights include the Plaça Abat Oliba (where local farmers sell honey and cheese) and, of course, the **monastery church** itself. A massive gateway (1942–68) leads to a modern inner courtyard, with the entrance to the monastery (locked) off to the left and also access to a 'holy spring'. To the right, a door leads into the transept of the church (Renaissance style, 1560–92) which leads on in turn to the famous *Madonna of Montserrat* above the altar. Pilgrims wait patiently in long queues to touch the 12th-century wooden figure, which has become blackened by candle-soot over the centuries. She is fondly referred to as *La Moreneta* ('the black-and-brown one'). Try not to miss the performances of traditional chorales (twice daily: 1pm, 6.45pm) given by the monastery's very own boys' choir.

There are several excellent hiking routes in the magnificent landscape surrounding the monastery. The Ermita Sant Miquel is 45 minutes away on foot, the Ermita de Sant Joan can be reached via cable ropeway and a 20-minute walk, and the summit of Sant Jeroni is directly accessible via cable car (the valley station is 3km/1 mile away on the road to Manresa).

Those with enough time on their hands at this stage should visit **Martorell** on the return journey, with its 'Devil's Bridge' and two interesting museums. Two other rewarding places to visit a bit further south are the wine centres of Vilafranca del Penedès (*Museu del Vi* wine museum: Tuesday to Sunday 10am–2pm and 4.30–7.30pm) and Sant Sadurní d'Anoia, where the famous Spanish champagne known as *cava* is produced (*see page 90*).

Sant Sadurní wine cellar

Route 2

Tarragona

Tarragona old town

Tarragona has the second-largest harbour in Catalonia, and the city is also the seat of an archbishop. The Romans had good reasons for making *Tarraco* the capital of their province of *Hispania Citerior*: the city is magnificently situated on a 70-m (230-ft) high hill right next to the sea.

History

The first settlers came from the Eastern Mediterranean. During the Second Punic War (218BC) the Romans, led by Gnaeus and Publius Scipio, conquered the city and then held it for over 400 years. *Tarraco* became their main base in the Western Mediterranean, and developed into an extremely prosperous city. A population of 30,000 greeted Caesar, Augustus and other emperors when they came to visit. There were temples, baths and palaces, and also an amphitheatre; fine villas were built in the suburbs.

The city experienced its heyday when it was *Julia Urbs Triumphalis Tarraconensis*, the capital of the Roman province of *Hispania Citerior*. When the Romans were forced to retreat before the Visigoth advance (AD416), however, the city gradually went into decline. The Moors, who arrived in 714, neglected the buildings completely. After Tarragona was conquered by Count Berenguer III of Barcelona in 1117 several of the ruins were rebuilt, but the city's former glory had been lost for ever. Barcelona became the centre of the new state of Catalonia.

City Tour

From the Rambla Vella, which today is the main traffic thoroughfare in the city, the Carrer Portalet leads to the

Remains of the Roman capital

Cathedral door-knocker and Gothic facade

Plaça de la Font ❶. On the western side of this square, which was once occupied by the Roman circus (340m/1,115ft x 110m/360ft), stands the New Town Hall. Follow the Carrer Misericòrdia uphill; it soon becomes the Carrer Major, and a few minutes later reaches the impressive flight of steps leading up to the ★ **Cathedral ❷**. This majestic basilica was built at the end of the 12th century, and was consecrated, though still incomplete, in 1331. The mighty Gothic portal (1278) is decorated with some fine sculpture representing the Virgin, the Apostles and the Prophets. Above them is the massive rose window. The narrower side portals and the unfinished bell-tower (65.5m/214ft high) are of Romanesque origin.

The entrance to the cathedral is through a side door to the left of the main portal. The ★ cloister is almost square, and is a fascinating mixture of Romanesque and Gothic. The most famous of the richly decorated capitals here is the one depicting the *Processio de les Rates*, in which rats can be seen leading a cat away to burial. At the eastern end of the cloister is the Diocesan Museum (July to October Monday to Saturday 10am–7pm, October to November 10am–5pm, November to March 10am–2pm, March to May 10am–1pm and 4–7pm). A Romanesque portal leads off the cloister into the cathedral proper, which measures 104m (340ft) x 54m (177ft). The left side-aisle of this solemn and impressive building contains seven chapels, among them the 14th-century Capilla dels Sastres ('Tailors' Chapel'), to the left of the main altar, with its alabaster altar to the Virgin.

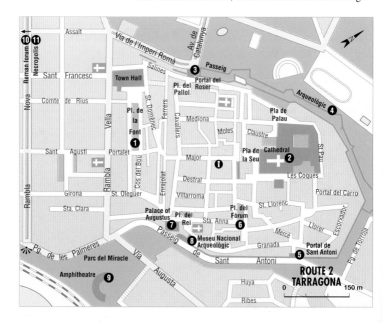

The choir dates from the 14th century and its exquisitely carved stalls (1479–89) are the work of Francisco Gomar. In the Capella Mayor there is a massive ★ high altar with an altarpiece (1426–34) by Pere Johan. His reliefs depict the life and trials of St Thekla, the patron saint of Tarragona. To the left of the altar is the marble tomb of the archbishop Juan de Aragón, who died in 1334; it is from the workshop of Andrea Pisano (1295–1349).

Altarpiece by Pere Joan

The nearby Plaça del Pallol, with its marvellous Gothic buildings, also contains the **Portal del Roser** ❸, the western gate of the old Roman city. This is the starting-point of the ★★ **Passeig Arqueològic** ❹ (winter: Monday to Saturday 9am–5pm, Sunday 10am–3pm; summer: Monday to Saturday 9am–9pm, Sunday 9am–3pm) an 'archaeology route' that leads along the former town wall and around the northern section of the Old Town, providing several excellent views of the city and the sea. The Roman wall was originally 4km (2 miles) long, and almost 10m (33ft) high in places; it was extended during the Middle Ages, and has a whole series of towers and gates.

Portal del Roser

From the end of the Passeig Arqueològic it's just a few minutes' walk to the **Portal de Sant Antoni** ❺, the old east gate. The **Plaça del Fòrum** ❻ used to be the Roman Forum, and measured 200m (650ft) x 300m (984ft). Current excavation work, which is being carried out in two phases, hopes to reveal an altar from the time of the Emperor Augustus. The narrow streets to the east of it (Carrer Santa Anna, Carrer Talavera, Carrer Portella) were the centre of the Jewish Quarter during medieval times. Today the Carrer Santa Anna contains the Museu d'Art Modern, with its contemporary painting and sculpture. The street leads on to the Plaça del Rei, with the eye-catching **Palace of Augustus** ❼ at its eastern end. This palace with its towers was originally built by Augustus and then later used as a royal residence.

Two tarraconenses

Part of the Roman collection

Shady old town alley

Next door to it is the famous ★★ **Museu Nacional Arqueològic** ❽ (winter: Tuesday to Saturday 10am–1.30pm and 4–7pm, Sunday 10am–2pm; summer and Easter: Tuesday to Saturday 10am–8pm, Sunday 10am–2pm). The museum contains many finds dating from Roman times: coins, ceramics, sarcophagi, busts and household implements of all kinds. The foundations of some Roman buildings have also been exposed to view in the basement. In the stairwell there is an enormous mosaic (4.5m/15ft x 6m/20ft) with various aquatic motifs, originally discovered at a Roman villa outside the city.

There are several more sights in Tarragona outside its Old Town. The Rambla Nova is a pedestrian precinct running parallel to the Rambla Vella. At its eastern end is the Balcó del Mediterrani with the memorial to admiral Roger de Llúria, who conquered Menorca in the 13th century. This balcony affords a magnificent view of the sea 35m (114ft) below and the tiny municipal beach, Platja del Miracle. T o the left are the remains of the old Roman **amphitheatre** ❾, which once seated 12,000 spectators. On the Carrer Lleida there are some ruins of an old **Roman forum** ❿ and a Roman theatre. A Roman **necropolis** ⓫ has been discovered on the Passeig de la Independència with more than 2,000 graves, dating from the 3rd–5th centuries AD. The Museu Paleocristià has exhibitions documenting the excavations, and adjoins the Necròpolis Romana.

4km (2 miles) north, towards Lleida, is the **Roman aqueduct**. Built during the reign of Trajan (AD98–117), its dimensions are very impressive: the upper row of arches is 217m (711ft) long, the lower row 73m (239ft), and it is 29m (95ft) high. In the town of Constantí, 5km (3 miles) north of here, the **Mausoleum of Centcelles**, now a museum, is worth visiting for its mosaics commissioned by a wealthy Roman landowner during the 4th century AD.

Route 3

Girona

Girona from the Onyar

Girona has a population of 90,000 and is situated 70m (230ft) above sea-level. Capital of the province of Girona, which takes in the entire Costa Brava, the city is an important trading centre, and has been the seat of a bishop since time immemorial. Four rivers run through the city, the largest is the Riu Ter; the smaller Riu Onyar, Riu Güell and Riu Galligants all flow into it. The area known as the New Town is situated between the Riu Ter and the Riu Onyar; it contains three main squares, the Plaça d'Espanya, Plaça d'Europa and Plaça dels Països Catalans. The well-preserved Old Town to the north of the Riu Onyar, with its charming streets, is a very worthwhile place to visit.

History

The town dates back to an Iberian settlement of the 5th century BC. It later became *Gerunda* under the Romans, and lay on their important transport route between the Pyrenees and Tarragona. In AD713 the Moors took it and renamed it *Djerunda*, but soon lost it again in 785 to Charlemagne. In the 9th century the town fell into the hands of the counts of Barcelona, and their union with the kingdom of Aragón in 1134 marked the high point of the city's fortunes. Nevertheless, Girona's strategically favourable location meant that it was regularly subjected to lengthy sieges. In 1285 King Philip III of France did his best to penetrate the ring of fortifications around the city – to no avail. Over the centuries that followed, Girona was besieged on 34 different occasions, each time unsuccessfully. In 1809 a French army of 35,000 men tried to starve the city into submission, but the small garrison under the command of General Alvarez de Castro still managed to stand up to the might of Napoleon for a full seven months. After that Girona remained under French control until 1814.

City Tour

A tour of the picturesque ★★ **Old Town** of Girona is best started at the **Pont de Pedra ❶**. This 'stone bridge' is quite unique: the pretty little bridges that span the Riu Onyar further to the west are all made of wood. On the left directly after the bridge, the Rambla de la Llibertat branches off; it is the central meeting-point in the city, day and night. From the Plaça del Vi, go down the Carrer Ciutadans. Just before the Plaça de l'Oli on the left is the triple-windowed facade of the **Fontana d'Or ❷**, a patrician's house with a fascinating mixture of Late

Waterfront tenements hide the old town

Romanesque and Gothic elements (the rear of the building is also worth a quick look, as is the Gothic loggia in its residential section).

The atmospheric Jewish quarter of **El Call ❸** begins at the Plaça de l'Oli. From the 9th century until they were expelled in 1492, many Jews lived in the narrow streets around the Carrer Força, where a narrow alley leads to the old ghetto and **Museu d'Història dels Jueus de Catalunya** (Monday to Saturday October to May 10am–6pm, May to October 10am–8pm, Sunday 10am–3pm). From the square a flight of steps leads uphill to the 17th-century Jesuit church of Sant Martí. A further flight of steps leads up to the Plaça Sant Domènec, with the facade of the old **monastery of Sant Domènec ❹** (Gothic church, cloister) at its eastern end. Also on this square are the remains of the old university, which was founded in 1443. The Renaissance facade with the Habsburg coat-of-arms is a reminder of its heyday between the 16th and 18th centuries, when Girona was the centre of learning in Catalonia. The city lost its claim to a university after its subjugation by Philip V during the War of the Spanish Succession. The Carrer Alemanys leads up further to the remains of the old city wall and the **Passeig Arqueològic**, a sightseeing route that leads around the northern part of the Old Town. There's a fantastic all-round view of the Old Town and the land beyond it from the top of the former watchtower, the *Torre Gironella*, and the walls.

The narrow street of San Cristòfol leads downhill past the mighty apse of the cathedral and into the Plaça dels Apòstols. The **Bishop's Palace ❺** is on the north side, its 12th-century facade connected to the cathedral by an arched gateway. The palace houses the **Museu d'Art** (Diocesan Museum, daily except Monday 10am–6pm, Sunday and public holidays 10am–2pm); special mention should be made of the 12th-century Romanesque frescoes

Jewish museum exhibit

Passeig Archeològic

from Pedrinya on display, and also the Gothic altars by Lluís Borrassà and Pedro Fontaines.

A magnificent flight of stone steps leads up to one of the finest sacred buildings in the whole of Catalonia, ★ **Girona Cathedral** ❻. Construction work on this superb basilica began in 1312 and took over four centuries to complete – and several architectural styles have consequently left their mark on it. The choir is predominantly Gothic, while the facade (1733) is Baroque. The single-aisled interior is 34m (110ft) high, 63m (200ft) long and a full 23m (75ft) wide, not including the chapels. This is a unique width for a Gothic nave. The three-aisled choir contains a fine Romanesque marble altar from the previous building, and the high altar has a 14th-century gilded retablo beneath a silver baldachin. Also worthy of note is the stone bishop's seat dating from the 11th century.

The Cathedral's south portal

At the side door entrance is the ★★ **Museu Capitular de la Catedral** (Cathedral Museum, Tuesday to Saturday 10am–noon and 4–6pm, July and August 10am–8pm, Sunday 10am–2pm), with its fine collection of ecclesiastical treasures. Highlight is the 12th-century ★★*Tapestry of the Creation*, a very well-preserved work showing Christ at the centre of 31 panels depicting the story of the Creation; there is also the illuminated 10th-century ★ *Commentary on the Apocalypse*, written in 975 by Beatus of Liébana, and one of the most precious books in Catalonia. Next to the museum is the Romanesque cloister with its double columns, and friezes depicting Biblical scenes.

33

At the foot of the steps outside the cathedral, go through the 14th-century Sobreportes town gate. On the left beyond it is the church of **Sant Feliu** ❼. It contains eight Roman and Early Christian sarcophagi set into the walls next to the altar. The magnificent Narcissus Chapel (1782), dedicated to the city's patron, Sant Narcís, is also worthy of note. Proceed now along the Carrer Ferran el Catòlic to the **Banys Arabs** ❽ (Arab Baths: Tuesday to Saturday 10am–7pm, Sunday 10am–2pm; winter Tuesday to Saturday 10am–2pm), which were built not by Arabs but by Christians, on the ruins of a Moorish bath-house in 1295.

Christ Jacent, Sant Feliu

Banys Arabs

On the other side of the Riu Galligants, the former monastery of **Sant Pere de Galligants** ❾, begun in 1131, houses the city's Archaeological Museum (Tuesday to Saturday 10am–1.30pm and 4–7pm, October to June 10am–2pm and 4–6pm, Sunday and public holidays 10am–2pm). With examples of Greek and Roman pottery, and some Jewish gravestones, but the rest of the collection is at the Museu d'Història dels Jueus.

Opposite the monastery is the small 12th-century church of Sant Nicolau, where temporary exhibitions are held. And a little further up the hill, laid out charmingly among the ruins of the old city wall, is a park in honour of John Lennon.

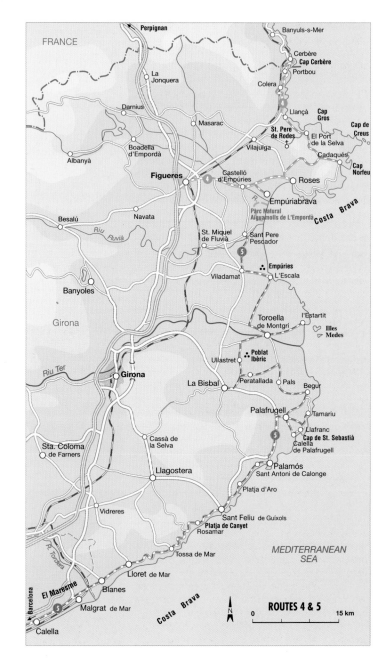

34

ROUTES 4 & 5

0   15 km

Route 4

The Land of Salvador Dalí

Portbou – Cadaqués – Figueres (75km/46 miles)

The northern section of the Costa Brava, which begins at Portbou on the Franco-Spanish border, is very wild and rocky. Some of the picturesque coves can only be reached by boat or on foot. The famous Surrealist painter and performance artist Salvador Dalí was born in this part of Catalonia, and traces of his creativity can be found all over it: in the idyllically situated fishing village of Cadaqués, for instance, or in the artist's birthplace of Figueres with its impressive Dalí Museum. Allow a week to explore this region.

Directly beyond the border there's a great view of the bay of **Portbou** (pop. 2,400) from the summit of the Col des Balitres (173m/567ft). It's hard to miss the massive and not very attractive railway station here, sprawled out across the slope above the town; it was built in 1929 so that train passengers arriving from France could step into Spanish trains, which needed broader tracks. Since the 1980s the gauge has been altered automatically for most modern trains, and if you travel with the Talgo or an EC train, there's no longer any need to change.

Portbou market and boulevard

Portbou has a narrow pebble beach with a small promenade. The old part of the town below the station is worth a quick visit. The cemetery at Portbou contains the grave of the German-Jewish aesthetician Walter Benjamin, the most important German literary critic of the 20th century. He committed suicide here on 27 September 1940, while on the run from the Gestapo, out of fear that the Spanish authorities would hand him over. A stairway leading nowhere by artist Dani Karavan symbolises the desperation that drove Benjamin to his death.

From Portbou the N-260 winds its way southwards along the steep coast. Past Grifeu, turn left to **Llançà** (pop. 3,000). The centre of the village, Llançà Vila, lies inland and was mentioned as *Villa Lancio* as far back as the 10th century, when it belonged to the nearby monastery of Sant Pere de Rodes *(see page 36)*. The beaches and the harbour, which lie 1km (¾ mile) further east, are popular weekend destinations for people from nearby Figueres.

Not far away, in the bay of Cap Gros, is ★ **El Port de la Selva** (pop. 900), a small and very picturesque fishing village famed for its delicious *anxoves* (anchovies), which should definitely be sampled in one of the numerous fish restaurants here. The magnificent beach is

El Port de la Selva

Sant Pere de Rodes

extremely popular with windsurfers. El Port de la Selva is also a good starting-point for exciting excursions: a boat trip along the rocky coast to the Cap de Creus, for instance, the easternmost point of the Iberian peninsula.

The former Benedictine monastery of ★★ **Sant Pere de Rodes** (winter: Tuesday to Sunday 10am–5.10pm, Tuesday free; summer: Tuesday to Sunday 10am–7.40pm) still exudes majesty and grandeur even though it's a ruin. It can either be reached on foot from El Port de la Selva, or by car via Vilajuiga. The ruined monastery is one of the most important examples of Romanesque and Mozarabian architecture in the whole of Catalonia. The location was mentioned as early as AD604; the monastery itself dates from 943, and its church from 1022. The whole place looks really forbidding, an impression strengthened by the square defensive tower, devoid of windows, and the bell-tower with its acoustic arcades. Inside the three-aisled church, note the fine Early Romanesque barrel vault, and the capitals ornamented with animal heads. The monastery fell into disuse at the beginning of the 19th century. A short hike from the monastery (about 15 minutes) lies the ruined castle of **San Salvador**, 670m (2,200ft) above sea level, with fine views out to sea.

Boat with tree: outside Dalí's house in Cadaqués

From El Port de la Selva the road winds inland towards the peak of Puig Pani (613m/2,011ft); during the descent in the direction of Cadaqués the bends become increasingly sharp. Roughly 5km (3 miles) further on, one of the most picturesque villages on the Costa Brava comes into view: ★★ **Cadaqués**. Many artists – Magritte, Buñuel and García Lorca, to name just a few – spent part of their lives in this charming fishing village and have retained its unique atmosphere and environment in their work. The village's most important inhabitant, however, was undoubtedly Salvador Dalí, who had a not entirely conventional villa, complete with eggs on the roof, built for himself and his wife Gala in the part of Cadaqués known as **Port Lligat**, 15 minutes' walk north of the centre. It has been turned into a museum, the **Casa-Museu Salvador Dalí** (June to September daily 10am–9pm, October–June daily 10.30am–6pm).

Port Lligat

Although the mainly stony beaches of Cadaqués aren't among the most attractive on the Costa Brava, the village is crowded during high season. It's particularly popular with young people, attracted by the nightlife, who come here to see and be seen. The old part contains little restaurants and pubs (Dalí having been no stranger to most of them), and there are several galleries and shops around the church of Santa Maria, which contains a magnificent baroque altar dating from 1727. Excursions into the surrounding area are very worthwhile; try a 6km (3 mile) hike to the **Cap de Creus** with its lighthouse and weird rock formations, or walk across to some of the more remote coves like S'Aranella, Del Ros, etc.

Cap de Creus

37

The next town along the coast, **Roses** (pop. 9,000), is separated from Cadaqués by a ridge of hills. Founded by the Greeks in the 8th century BC, when it was known as *Rhode*, the town later became a fortified harbour under the Visigoths, and then the seat of the Counts of Empúries. Today the town lives off fishing and tourism. Its fine beaches have made it the most popular tourist centre of the entire northern Costa Brava, and it's also much frequented by divers and yachtsmen. Although the town centre contains rather a lot of modern high-rise hotels, there are numerous archaeological remains somewhat further out of town. These include: the 16th-century citadel with the remains of a Benedictine monastery and the Romanesque basilica of Santa María (1022); the ruined 17th-century Castel de la Trinidad with its magnificent view of the Golf de Roses; the Puig Rom peak (229m/750ft, probably the site of the Visigoth settlement); and the dolmen graves of Creu d'en Corbetella.

The 'lagoon estate' of **Empúriabrava** was only built in the 1970s. It is a town created exclusively for (mostly German) tourists, with around 70,000 visitors in the summer but only 6,000 or so in winter. The buildings are grouped around an extensive network of artificial canals, guaranteeing that every inhabitant can sail right up to his or her front door. There is also a marina and a small airport. The construction of this estate did have one positive effect: in 1976 various environmentally-minded local people decided to form an action group, whose persistence resulted in the creation of the nature reserve known as ★★ **Aiguamolls de L'Empordà**. It surrounds Empúriabrava and largely

Empúriabrava

Castelló Cathedral: the alabaster altarpiece, witness to many vows

ensures that the fauna and flora of this marshy area can flourish undisturbed, away from the intrusions of tourism.

The town of **Castelló d'Empúries** (pop. 2,000) has lost quite a lot of its former glory, but it still boasts the very impressive Gothic cathedral of Santa Maria (13th–15th centuries), with its Romanesque tower. It is the second largest cathedral in the province after the one in Girona, and contains a magnificent alabaster altarpiece (1485) by Vicento Borrás among others, and also a Gothic retable. Other sights worth seeing here include the former stock exchange (Casa de la Vila, on the Plaça dels Homes), the seven-arched Gothic bridge across the Riu Muga, and the Museu Farinera c/Sant Francesc, 5 a flour-milling factory still in operation.

The next stop is **Figueres** (pop. 30,000), the economic centre of the *comarca* of Alt Empordà. This honest working town is a real treasure trove for art lovers. It began as a medieval settlement close to today's centre, which used to be part of the monastery of Sant Pere de Rodes. Figueres received its royal charter in 1267, during the reign of Jaume I. The Count of Empúries, Hugo IV, disagreed with this formal misappropriation on behalf of the king, and set fire to the town in 1274. Nothing much happened for several hundred years after that until Figueres suddenly experienced an economic upswing in the 18th century because of wine and maize exports. This moved Fernando VII to construct a massive series of fortifications along the outside of the city, known as the Castell de Sant Ferran.

At the centre of the town is its small *Rambla*. At the eastern end of the square is a monument to the inventor Narcís Monturiol (1810–85), a native of Figueres who developed one of the earliest submarines. There are also two interesting museums on the Rambla: house No 2 contains the **Museu de l'Empordà** (July to September Tuesday to Saturday 9am–7pm, October to June Tuesday to Saturday 11am–7pm, Sunday 11am–2pm), which has archaeological finds from the region, and paintings and watercolours by contemporary Catalan artists. At the old Hotel de Paris in the Rambla is the **Museu del Joguet de Catalunya**, an excellent toy museum (10am–1pm, 4–7pm).

Go uphill now from the Rambla to reach the town's main attraction, the ★★ **Teatre-Museu Dalí** (October to June Tuesday to Sunday 10.30am–5.45pm, July to September daily 9am–7.45pm) on the Plaça Gala-Salvador Dalí. During the 1980s, the world-famous artist set up the museum himself in Figueres' 19th-century theatre, which had been ruined in the Civil War and left empty. Dalí was very fond of the building – he had staged his first exhibition there at the age of 14. He gave it an enormous glass dome, and turned it into an impressive temple of his art.

Salvador Dalí was born in Figueres on 11 May 1904. In 1922 he went to Madrid to study at the School of Fine Art and met García Lorca and Luis Buñuel there, but just three years later he was so homesick he returned to Catalonia. He did his military service in the Castell de Sant Ferran in Figueres. In 1929 he met his future wife, Gala, and followed her to Paris. Regarding himself as a 'Catalonian farmer', the artist soon returned to his homeland and bought a small fishing hut for himself and Gala at Port Lligat *(see page 37)*, which he extended. He spent the Civil War and World War II in the USA, where he became an acclaimed fashion designer – but in 1948 he was back in Port Lligat. Ten years later he married Gala in the church of Els Angels near Girona, and from then on he left Catalonia only rarely. Dalí built the Castell Gala Dalí for his princess and she is buried here. More surrealist sculptures in the gardens (same timetable as Museu Dalí). Embittered after his wife's death, he spent the final years of his life in the Torre Galatea near his museum in Figueres. He died in 1989.

In the courtyard of his museum, visitors are greeted by Dalí's wife and muse, Gala, in a black Cadillac, before being drawn further and further into the weird and distorted world of the Surrealist. There is an altar made of liqueur bottles; a living room designed as a *Homage to Mae West*; and everywhere there are those fascinating paintings of Dalí's where everything seems to be oozing and flowing. The burial chamber in the museum, which contains the 'divine' artist, is modest in comparison.

A third Dalí museum is in the medieval **castle of Pubol** south of Figueres (Easter to Nov 1, 10am–6pm, closed Mon). This beautiful building contains Gala's wardrobe as well as furniture and paintings by Dalí.

Dalí's Homage to Mae West and the black Cadillac

Route 5

Along the Coast

**Sant Pere Pescador – Palamós – Blanes – Barcelona
(179km/111 miles)** *See map on page 34*

The coastline is flat for much of this route. The road only starts getting serpentine after Sant Feliu de Guíxols, when the Costa Brava shows its 'wild' face once again. L'Escala gives a fascinating glimpse into Greek and Roman history, and its beaches are also justifiably famous. The last section of the route crosses the very touristy and hence rather less attractive region known as *El Maresme*, which is officially no longer part of the Costa Brava. Several days are needed for a thorough exploration of the southern section of the Costa Brava.

*Good swimmming around
San Pere Pescador*

Anchovies in L'Escala

The small town of **Sant Pere Pescador** (pop. 2,000) not only contains the remains of an old fort and a 17th-century baroque church, it also has quite a good beach a few kilometres to the east of its centre which is growing increasingly popular with windsurfers.

The nearby fishing harbour at **L'Escala** (pop. 4,000) is one of the largest in the region. While it has lost some of its importance in recent years, its reputation for salted anchovies continues, though most of them are not caught here. The town has little to offer as far as historical sights are concerned, apart from a neoclassical seamen's cemetery, and the mariners' monument at the tip of the La Punt promontory. There are some good beaches, including the Cala Montgó to the south, the Platja de Riells, and the Platja d'Empúries to the north. There is also a marina in the neighbouring village of La Clota.

Just 2km (1 mile) to the north of L'Escala is the site of the ancient Greek town of *Emporion*, today known as ★ **Empúries** (daily 10am–8pm, October to June 10am–6pm), the most remarkable archaeological site on the Costa Brava. By the way, it's best to allow at least half a day for any visit here. The museum at the entrance is a good place to get one's bearings before venturing out across the excavations.

The most ancient section of this fascinating site, to the north, is known as the 'Old Town' *(Palaiopolis)*. It was founded in the 6th century by Greek settlers from Asia Minor and originally lay on an island. The ruins of the Late Gothic church of **Sant Martí** were probably built above a Greek temple to Artemis. There used to be a small harbour below *Palaipolis*; it gradually became land, and the town of Sant Martí d'Empúries was built above it during the Middle Ages. An 85-m (278-ft) long **mole** still survives from the old Greek harbour; it was built between 175BC and 150BC.

Empúries: the Palaiopolis

To the south of the old harbour the Greeks built a 'New Town' *(Neapolis)* when *Palaiopolis* had been outgrown after only a few decades. The remains of the Cyclopean wall (ca 250BC) are well-preserved, eg the **south gate**, which was formerly the main entrance to the town. To the right of it is the **Temple of Jupiter Serapis** (ca 100BC), covering a ground area of 45m/147ft x 24m/78ft and formerly enclosed by a Doric colonnade. To the left are sections of the **Temple of Asklepios**, with a statue of the Greek god of healing. The former main street leads to the **market place** *(agora)*, which measures 60m/196ft x 22m/72ft; on the edge of it are the ruins of an **assembly hall** *(stoa)* dating from the 3rd century BC, and the remains of a **Christian basilica** erected by the Visigoths in the 6th century AD.

Temple of Jupiter Serapis

To the west of *Neapolis* are the remains of a Roman town built after the area was occupied by the Roman commander Scipio the Elder (218BC). It flourished during the 1st and 2nd centuries BC. The ruins of two **Roman villas** can be admired here: note the well-preserved mosaics and also the basin for collecting rainwater *(impluvium)*. At the centre of the Roman settlement is the **forum**, and south of it are the **south gate**, part of Caesar's massive town wall, and the **amphitheatre**.

The next destination on this route is **Torreolla de Montgrí** (pop. 5,500), dominated by the 300m- (985ft-) high rocky outcrop of Santa Catarina (which has a small hermitage on top), and by the Castell de Montgrí. This castle on the summit of the 'grey mountain' *(Montgrí)* was erected in 1294 by King Jaume II as a defence against the counts of nearby Empúries. The mighty structure with its round towers takes about an hour to reach on foot from

Torreolla's Plaça de la Vila

Torreolla street advertisement

The protected Illes Medes

the town. The interior is closed to visitors, but there's still a very rewarding view for those who make the climb.

The best place to start a tour of the town itself is at the **Plaça de la Vila**, a pretty square surrounded by arcades, with the 14th-century Town Hall and the small 13th-century church of Sant Antoni. To the north of the square, in the Carrer de l'Església, is the Palau Solterra (now the Fundació Vila-Casas with a Catalan modern art public collection), one of several palazzos dating from the Renaissance period, and a short distance further on is the 15th-century single-aisled Gothic church, which was radically restored during the 19th century. The old part of the town is enclosed by a wall, and two of the former six gates are still in existence: the Torre de Santa Catalina and the Torre de les Bruixes. A glimpse into the history of the town and the surrounding region is provided by the **Can Quintana** (c/Vllá 31 Monday to Saturday 11am–2pm and 5pm–8pm Sundays 11am–2pm).

Around 6km (4 miles) to the east of Torreolla is the tourist centre of **L'Estartit** (pop. 1,000), which was originally the town's harbour. The most noticeable feature here is the broad beach with its fine sand extending across several kilometres. Protected from harsh winds by a nearby range of hills, this beach with its shallow water is ideal for children. Apart from the ruins of its old town gate, L'Estartit has little to offer from the historical point of view, but there's a great variety of tourist activities. The long promenade has rows of restaurants, stores, and diving and windsurfing shops, and there's also a miniature railway that does round trips along the coast. Although the town receives tens of thousands of visitors every year, it's very quiet at night.

The ★ **Illes Medes** are the main attraction at L'Estartit. They're a group of seven small islands offshore, which formerly served as a hideaway for pirates. Today the islands are a sanctuary for rare birds and plants. Since the mid-1980s they have been a nature reserve, and are now closed to visitors. Even divers are only allowed to come within a maximum of 75m (250ft) of this natural paradise.

The small village of **Ullastret**, roughly 20km (12 miles) away from L'Estartit, is famous for the nearby Iberian settlement of **Poblat Ibèric**, founded in the 7th century BC on an island in a lake (now silted up). Over the centuries the settlement gradually received some impressive rampart fortifications on its western side, of which several sections – including six round towers – remain. The Iberians here traded a great deal with the Greeks in Emporion *(see page 41)*. The settlement went into decline during the 2nd century BC, probably due to the rapid growth of nearby Roman Empúries. A museum (June to October Tuesday

Pals' medieval centre

to Sunday 10am–8pm, October to May Tuesday to Sunday 10am–6pm, 2pm and 3pm) has been set up here, containing sketches and models of the excavation site, and also ceramics, coins, skulls and other finds.

Roughly 10km (6 miles) to the south of Ullastret is the town of **La Bisbal** (pop. 7,500). The town is especially famous for its ceramics; the craft has been practised here since the 15th century, and colourful ceramic wares are on sale in several shops. Other interesting sights here include the double-arched medieval bridge across the Riu Daró and the 15th-century palace of the bishops of Girona.

Unhurried La Bisbal

The route goes eastwards now, back towards the sea, and passes through the small, picturesque village of **Peratallada**, which is worth a visit. Time seems to have stopped for good here, just beyond the little stone bridge, and the narrow alleys and ornate houses are a real delight. The castle of 'hewn stone' *(petra tallada)*, was first mentioned as long ago as 1065. It is now a hotel and restaurant.

Peratallada castle

The busy market town of **Pals** (pop. 1,800) is 7km (4 miles) from the sea. The real highlight here is the medieval centre, which lies on a small rise at some distance from the road and can only be entered on foot. Two interesting sights here are the Romanesque church (with 15th-century Gothic additions) and the Torre de les Hores. The latter, which has had a clock since the 15th century (hence its name 'tower of the hours') was originally part of a medieval castle. From its base there is a fine view of the surrounding landscape as far as the Illes Medes *(see page 42)*. The **Ca la Pruna**, a 16th-century fortified house outside the town walls, contains a small municipal museum (1 July to 30 September daily 10.30am–1.30pm and 5.30–8.30pm, winter weekends only).

There is a really good view out across the sea from **Begur** (pop. 2,500), which is situated 200m (650ft) above

The rugged coast at Begur

Sant Martí in Palafrugell

Delightful Llafranc

the steep coastline. Distinctive features of Begur are its ruined 15th-century castle and also its medieval watchtowers, which served as a defence against pirates. Two kilometres (1 mile) to the north of Begur are the fine beaches of Sa Riera, Aiguafreda and Sa Tuna. A short distance to the south are the attractive beaches of Fornells and Aiguablava (and the nearby rock caves of Cova d'en Gisbert and Cova del Bisbe).

About 8km (5 miles) south of Begur is the commercial and economic centre of the region, **Palafrugell** (pop. 17,000). The town is also famous as the birthplace of Catalan writer Josep Pla (1897–1981). His house can be visited at c/Nou 49–51. Cork processing has been one of the town's most important industries for a long time now. Apart from its Gothic parish church of **Sant Martí** and some art nouveau buildings (eg the Armstrong Cork Factory, 1904), Palafrugell does not have much to offer as far as historical sights are concerned. There's the Museu dal Suro at Tarongeta 31, documenting the history of cork processing (Tuesday to Saturday 10am–1pm, 5–9pm, Sunday 10.30am–1.30pm).

For tourists seeking relaxation, however, the beach resorts near Palafrugell are an attractive proposition. **Tamariu, Llafranc** and **Calella** are all easily accessible. The little bay of Tamariu – named after the many tamarind trees here – is also a good place to fish as well as swim. Those who feel like doing more than just lying on the 500-m (1,640-ft) long sandy beach should go on an excursion to the nearby Cap de Sant Sebastià, with its baroque church and hermitage. The hotel and restaurant El Far is very romantic. Cap Roig is also worth a visit: its marvellous Jardí Botànic de Cap Roig (daily 9am–8pm summer, 9am–6pm winter), stretching down to the sea, was laid out by a White Russian emigré officer in the 1920s, and contains a wealth of plants native to the Mediterranean.

Further along the coast, the next main town after Palafrugell is **Palamós** (pop. 12,500). Founded in 1277, this town had its heyday during the Middle Ages when its harbour was the main base for the Aragonese fleet, which penetrated the Mediterranean as far as Sicily. Later, Palamós went into decline and only experienced an economic upswing in the 19th century when the cork industry developed here. The town is still the main export harbour for the products of the so-called 'cork triangle' (Palafrugell, Palamós and Sant Feliu de Guixols). Tourism is becoming increasingly important, too. Sights worth seeing in Palamós include the **Museu de la Pesca Port de Palamós** (winter: Tuesday to Saturday 10am–1.30pm, 3–7pm, Sundays 10am–2pm and 4–7pm; summer: Tuesday to Saturday 11am–9pm) with its collections of Iber-

ian, Greek and Roman ceramics and exhibits on local cork production, and the church of **Santa Maria** which was begun in 1371 and renovated in the 16th century. Alongside its municipal beach and palm-lined promenade, the resort of Palamós also has several other good beaches to the north (Platja de la Fosca, Platja de Castell) and to the west near Sant Antoni de Calonge.

Palamós promenade and statuary at Santa Maria

45

Beyond Sant Antoni de Calonge is the small town of **Platja d'Aro** (pop. 3,000) with its endless beach and hotel high-rise skyline right next to the water's edge. The night-life is noisy, the beaches are crowded and the shopping streets rather uninspiring, but outside the town there are several interesting historical sights. Castell d'Aro, 3km (1¾ miles) away, is the seat of the local administration and has an 11th-century church as well as a medieval castle, the Castell de Benedormiens; or there is also Romanyà de la Selva, 10km (6 miles) to the west, with its 4,000-year-old necropolis known as Cova d'en Daina. Of the dolmen graves that still survive there is an interesting passageway tomb made of stone slabs piled above each other, and also a stone circle *(cromlech)*.

Platja d'Aro before the rush

Continue along the coast southwestwards with the sea on your left. The route passes a turn-off to S'Agaró, a cosmopolitan beach resort for the wealthy with some magnificent villas, before arriving at **Sant Feliu de Guíxols** (pop. 16,500). This resort was once the most important tourist centre on the Costa Brava, but has now ceded precedence to Lloret de Mar, roughly 30km (18 miles) away. One positive aspect is that the town is almost completely free of ugly concrete high-rise hotels and noisy discotheques. Indeed, life along the promenade and near the little beach is almost tranquil. Very close by (Plaça del Monestir) are the ruins of a former Benedictine monastery,

Along the Costa Brava corniche

Tossa de Mar: bays and cafés

the reason for the town's existence. The monastery is said to have been founded by Charlemagne in 785 (the 10th century is more likely) in honour of St Felix who drowned here; only the 14th-century monastery church and the 10th-century Iron Gate *(Porta Ferrada)* still survive.

A road leads roughly 2km (1 mile) from the southern side of the harbour promenade up to the pilgrimage church of Ermita Sant Elm, where there's a superb view of the town and the rocky coastline below. It's also worth taking a brief hike (5km/3 miles) inland at this point to the rock known as La Pedralta – it has a cross on top and actually seems to be floating in mid-air – and then on to the Capella Sant Baldiri.

The ★★ **road** between Sant Feliu de Guíxols and Tossa de Mar is one of the finest along the entire Costa Brava. For 22km (13 miles) the well-paved road follows a series of hairpins up to a height of almost 600m (2,000ft), providing a continual series of stunning views of the sea crashing on to the rocks far below. Inland, the road is lined by pine-trees and cork oak forests, and several gravel roads – some of them unsuitable for cars – lead to various hidden bays and coves, e.g. the Platja de Canyet near Rosamar, the Cala de Salións near Salións or the Cala Bona shortly before Tossa. The road finally winds its way down into the impressive bay of ★ **Tossa de Mar** (pop. 3,300).

Tossa, or *Turissa* as it was known to the Romans, has always been a popular place with artists because of its superb natural setting: Marc Chagall immortalised in a series of unforgettable paintings, some of which can be admired in the small municipal museum (Tuesday to Sunday 11am–1pm and 3–5pm, in summer 10am–9pm) in the old part of the town.

The pride and joy of Tossa de Mar is Vila Vella, its Old Town, situated on a promontory. The ruins of an old Roman settlement dating from the 1st century BC can be found here, as well as sections of the old medieval town wall which still has three of its original four fortified towers. Narrow streets containing galleries, small cafés and restaurants lead up to the top of the hill, from where there is a fine view of the bay.

Unlike many other tourist centres along the Costa Brava, Tossa de Mar conveys a strong sense of architectural unity and harmony. Only a handful of high-rise hotels disturb the skyline. As well as its horseshoe-shaped beach, Platja Gran, from which boats leave for Blanes, Tossa also has several other beaches that are rather hard to reach: the tiny Platja del Reig to the north, and the Mar Menuda beach opposite the little island of L'Illa. The small beach of Es Codolar lies right at the foot of the Old Town to the south.

Sun blockers, Lloret de Mar

The town of **Lloret de Mar** (pop. 10,500), just 13km (8 miles) further on, is a real contrast to the tranquillity of Tossa, with its amusement arcades, discos, bars, etc. As many as 170 hotels, some of them utterly antiquated, await visitors from all over the world. Lloret is the Costa Brava's most popular package-tour destination, but there's little of historical interest here apart from the 16th-century parish church with its 20th-century art nouveau tiled chapel. The town does have a bit of Mediterranean flair outside peak season, however: its somewhat quieter bays away from the centre include the Platja de Fenals, or the bay of Santa Cristina a little further south with its Ermita of the same name. The **Jardí Pinya de Rosa** (daily 9am–6pm year round), a 'branch' of the Mar i Murtra botanical garden in Blanes *(see below)*, is just a few minutes' walk from here. Also interesting is Jardi de Santa Clotilde, a rennaisance garden (May to October Tuesday to Sunday 10am–1pm and 4–8pm).

The route continues another 6km (3½ miles) inland from Lloret to reach **Blanes** (pop. 21,000). Industry (cork, textiles, canning) as well as tourism is important for Blanes, but it has still preserved its charm, unlike Lloret. The old town has relatively few high-rise buildings; tourism has instead been concentrated along the beach at Passeig S'Abanell. Sights at Blanes include the hexagonal Gothic fountain on the Carrer Ample, commissioned by the Countess Cabrera in the 15th century, and the 14th-century church of Santa Maria, situated high above the Old Town, with its impressive baroque altar. The beach promenade is bounded to the northeast by a promontory extending into the sea, with the remains of the 11th-century Castell de Sant Joan (165m/540ft above sea-level, accessible on foot in about one hour).

Traditional boat

47

Lloret: the biggest resort

48

Below the castle, picturesquely situated and facing the sea, is the attractive ★ **Mar i Murtra** botanical garden (April to October, daily 9am–6pm, October to April 10am–5pm Monday to Friday, weekends 10am–2pm; bus connection from the harbour to the entrance every 10 minutes). The garden was laid out originally by a German, Karl Faust (1874–1952), in 1920. Over the decades a fascinating collection of Mediterranean and North African flora has developed here.

Blanes is the southernmost town on the Costa Brava. The Riu Tordera marks the boundary between the provinces of Girona and Barcelona, and the following section of coastline, El Maresme, differs from the Costa Brava in many ways, not just geographically.

El Maresme

From Malgrat de Mar onwards the road hugs the coast, running parallel to the Girona-Barcelona railway line. Many of the local inhabitants are thus obliged to use bridges or underpasses to reach the beaches, which are mostly man-made, and are continually being swept away by the currents. The narrow strip of coast here bears no comparison with the rocky coastline of the Costa Brava; the only visual relief is provided by the odd enormous hotel or concrete skyscraper. And yet this strip of coast still attracts hundreds of thousands of holidaymakers, most of them Germans (hence its nickname: _Costa de los Alemanes_). Tourists from abroad have to share their narrow beaches with weekend visitors from nearby Barcelona, who ensure that the road is always utterly congested on Friday afternoons and Sunday evenings. Tourism is not the only important source of revenue to have established itself in the area: just inland from the coast vegetables and flowers are grown in enormous greenhouses for the markets of Barcelona.

With all the tourism it comes as no surprise that the ancient centres of small towns such as Pineda de Mar, Calella de la Costa, Canet de Mar or Arenys de Mar are now virtually non-existent. One exception, however, is **Mataró** (pop. 10,000), birthplace of the Modernist architect Puig i Cadafalch (1867–1957, _see page 85_). Its medieval basilica of Santa Maria has a fine baroque interior, and the Casa Coll i Regàs (Carrer d'Argentona 55), which was built in 1893, is a good example of late 19th-century Catalonian art nouveau. The odd section of Roman _Lluro_ (e.g. the Torre Llauder) survives here and there, too. Greater Barcelona _(see page 14)_ really begins just beyond Mataró. Almost everyone in the towns of Vilasar, Premià de Mar and El Masnou works in the capital of Catalonia, and commutes daily. There are beaches along here, but they're permanently overcrowded.

Route 6

La Punta, Sitges

On the Trail of the Romans

Barcelona – Tarragona – Ebro Delta (205km/127 miles)
See map on page 50–1

49

This route starts off by following the northern part of the Costa Daurada as far as the Roman city of Tarragona *(see page 27)*. This northern section of the so-called 'Gold Coast' is far more varied and exciting than its southern part. The route then continues past farmland and large expanses of flat beach as far as the nature reserve of the Ebro Delta, with its fascinating flora and fauna. Allow several days for the whole trip, not including Tarragona.

Leave Barcelona, heading south along the C-31. The road soon crosses the delta of the Riu Llobregat and skirts a number of coastal marshes. Long before Castelldefels the coastal region is already built up, with enormous campsites and decrepit apartment houses blocking the view of the sea.

The 5-km (3-mile) long beach at **Castelldefels** (pop. 26,000) is popular, especially with weekend visitors from Barcelona. In the town itself the ruined 10th-century castle, the medieval watchtowers and the chapel are all worth a visit (the latter contains local archaeological finds and temporary exhibitions, and is a popular venue for concerts). Beyond Castelldefels the road winds its way up into the foothills of the mountain ridge known as the Massís de Garraf. Here, almost 300m (984ft) up, there is a fine view of the steep Costes del Garraf.

Sitges summer home

The next stop on the route is ★ **Sitges** (pop. 12,000), a resort with a long tradition of tourism, which is actually divided into two distinct sections by the rocky outcrop at its centre. In the southwest, the palm-lined beaches, dignified-looking hotels, marina and yacht clubs all bear witness to the golden '50s, when Sitges was very much an exclusive haunt of the wealthy. Today that image has grown somewhat tarnished, and beyond the beach the town has its predictable pedestrian precinct, discos and bars.

On the rocky outcrop known as La Punta are the first few buildings of the **Old Town**, such as the 18th-century baroque church with its late-Gothic altarpiece by Nicolau Credença (1499) dedicated to the town's patron saints, Bartholomew and Thekla. The **Museu Maricel** (Tuesday to Sunday 10am–2pm and 5–9pm; winter Tuesday to Friday 10am–1.30pm and 3–6.30pm, Saturday 10am–7pm Sunday 10am–3pm) is just a few steps away. The collection features Romanesque and Gothic paintings and also frescoes by Josep Maria Sert (1874–1945), who also did the interior decoration for the cathedral in Vic *(see page 71)*. Right next to the sea, the museum of **Cau Ferrat** (same times as Museu Maricel) is the former home of the writer and painter Santiago Rusiñol (1861–1931). Everything has been left exactly as it was during the artist's lifetime: there's a tiled fountain, some turn-of-the-century furniture, and several paintings not only by Rusiñol but by other famous names as well, including El Greco, Picasso and Utrillo.

The northwestern part of Sitges is relatively peaceful, and life generally proceeds at a leisurely pace. The town has made a name for itself as the location of the Sitges-

Coat of arms and tiles near Cau Ferrat

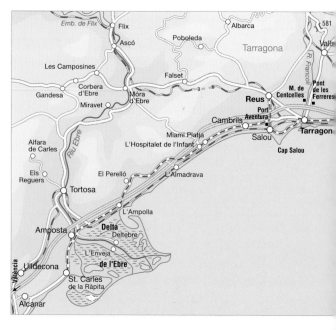

Barcelona veteran car rally, and is also famous for its Film Festival (held annually in October) and its 'International Theatre Festival' (held in May/June).

A popular local pursuit

Instead of visiting the Gran Casino de Barcelona in Sant Pere de Ribes (4km/2 miles away) it will be cheaper and more enjoyable to stroll through the streets of **Vilanova i la Geltrú** (pop. 40,000). Founded in 1070, today it's an industrial town with a very attractive old harbour quarter and several impressive historical sights such as the church of Santa Maria with its Renaissance altar, the 13th-century castle, the Roman excavations at the former settlement of *Darro*, and two interesting museums: the **Casa Papiol**, once residence of the painter Joaquim Mir, houses the Museum of 19th-Century Applied Art (Tuesday to Saturday 9.30am–2pm and 4–6pm, Sunday 9am–2pm); and the **Museu Balaguer** (Tuesday to Saturday 10am–1.30pm, 4.30–7pm, Thursday also 6–8.30pm, Sunday 10am–1.30pm; summer: Tuesday to Saturday 10am–2pm, 4.30–7.30pm, Thursday 6–9pm, Sunday 10am–2pm) contains paintings by Spanish masters of the 16th–19th centuries, and archaeological finds from the surrounding area.

South of Vilanova there are several small resorts with good beaches. Cubelles, a popular weekend haunt for people from Barcelona, is the last town in Barcelona province. The town after it, Cunit (2.5-km/1½-mile long sandy beach, Romanesque church) lies in the province of Tarragona.

51

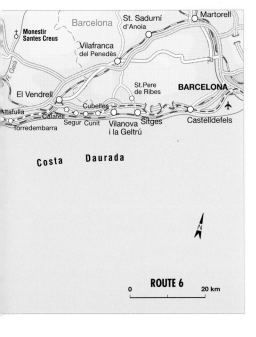

Casals remembered, El Vendrell

Beyond Segur de Calafell the road leads inland. From Calafell, head for **El Vendrell** (pop. 12,000). The town has been an important traffic junction since Roman times: the *Via Augusta* used to pass by here. To the south of El Vendrell are the beaches of Coma-ruga and Sant Salvador, where there is a memorial to the town's most famous son, the legendary cellist Pau (Pablo) Casals (1876–1973). His parents' house has been converted into a concert hall and small museum.

The route now continues on the trail of the Romans. Eight kilometres (5 miles) beyond El Vendrell we pass the Arc de Berà, a 12-m (39-ft) high triumphal arch built in the 2nd century AD on the Via Augusta connecting Gaul to Southern Spain; it was dedicated to Lucius Licinius Sura, a wealthy friend of Trajan. Before reaching the outskirts of Tarragona, the road passes through a series of former fishing communities that have since become tourist centres: Torredembarra, Altafulla and Tamarit. Six kilometres (4 miles) outside Tarragona it's worth making a detour inland to the **El Medól Quarry**. This is where the Romans quarried much of their construction material for nearby *Tarraco*. A monolith, known as L'Agulla de Médol, stands as a mute reminder of Tarragona's glorious past. For a detailed description of Tarragona, *see Route 2, page 27.*

The modern resort of Salou

South of Tarragona is the tourist centre of **Salou** (pop. 5,200). Charter buses arrive here daily from all over Europe, and the discotheques are also very popular with the young people of Tarragona and Reus. Salou was originally a Phoenician settlement, and later on, as *Salauris*, it became an important Roman harbour. The Aragonese fleet set sail from here on its Mediterranean sorties during medieval times. Little of the town's former glory remains today, however: the Torre Vella (1530) and the house known as Masia Catalana are exceptions. The main attractions are the two beaches of Platja Ponent and Platja Llevant, with their hotel high-rises, amusement centres and yachting harbours, and also **Port Aventura** north of the town centre, one of Europe's largest amusement parks. Visit Polynesia plus dancers, the Great Wall of China, Mexico (complete with pyramids), or a Wild West Saloon plus obligatory shootout. Water is the main means of transport: visitors travel along canals (July to September 10am–midnight; March to June and September to January 10am–8pm daily).

A rural ride

A country road winds its way across the marshy region filled with reeds near Salou as far as **Cambrils** (pop. 11,500). This former fishing village has retained much of its original charm. The old part of it is still intact, and the harbour promenade is still relatively free of concrete

Cambrils fishermen

additions. The bell-tower is particularly impressive; it was built as a defence against pirates in medieval times. The large yacht harbour here is well-known to mariners.

Just 4km (2½ miles) northwest of Cambril on the road to Montbrió del Camp is the **Parc Sama**, a garden with subtropical vegetation and plenty of art nouveau details. Surrounding an elegant villa, it was laid out at the end of the 19th century (daily 9am–9pm summer and 9am–6pm winter). The long, flat beaches of the Costa Daurada begin beyond Cambrils. Most of the seaside communities along it only sprang up during the past few decades.

Amposta (pop. 15,000) is the capital of Montsià, and Arabic influence here is very much in evidence, e.g. **La Cárrova** tower, built by the Moors. An enormous suspension bridge spans the Riu Ebre here. To the east of Amposta is a large promontory that becomes wider rather than narrower, the ★★ **Delta de L'Ebre**. Criss-crossed by a series of narrow roads, the delta is an important cultivation area for fruit and vegetables, especially rice, and since 1983 has been a nature reserve. Towards the sea the landscape is unspoilt, its sand dunes harbouring some unique fauna and flora. The delta is also a paradise for birds; over 300 different species inhabit the region permanently, including cormorants, flamingoes and herons. The main communities here are Deltebre and Sant Jaume d'Enveja, both connected via a car ferry that runs half-hourly. The fishing centre of **Sant Carles de la Ràpita** (pop. 10,000) is becoming increasingly popular with tourists, not least because of its picturesque location on the bay of Les Alfacs. The town is also famed for its seafood dishes.

The strip of coast known as the Costa del Azahar begins beyond Sant Carles; it belongs to the autonomous region of Valencia.

Torre de La Cárrova

View inland from the delta

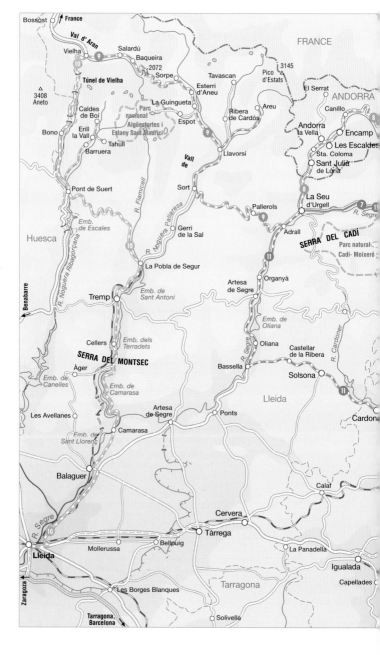

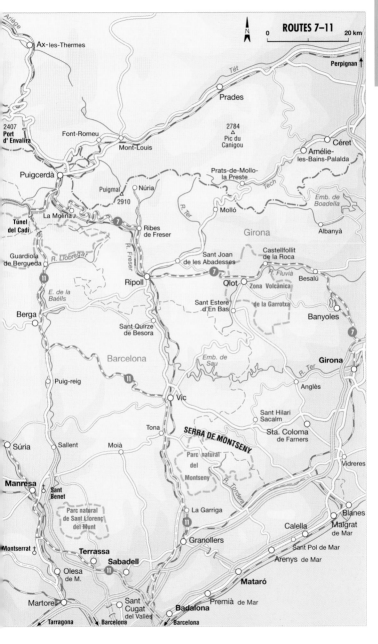

Route 7

In the Shadow of the Pyrenees

Girona – Banyoles – Ripoll – Puigcerdà – La Seu d'Urgell (202km/125 miles) *See map on pages 54–5*

This route leads along the lake of Banyoles, through the volcanic area of the Garrotxa region and up to the Benedictine monastery in Ripoll. Here, the Pyrenees begin to make their presence felt: the road to Puigcerdà winds its way up to a height of 1,800m (5,900ft). Those eager to reach La Seu d'Urgell or Andorra should plan an overnight stay. For a description of Girona, *see Route 3, page 31.*

Banyoles lake

Northwest of Girona is **Banyoles** (pop. 13,000). It lies on the shore of the lake of the same name, which is 2km (1 mile) long, 700m (2,295ft) wide and up to 40m (130ft) deep; the rowing championships of the 1992 Olympic Games were held here. The old part of Banyoles has several interesting historical sights, including the ruins of the former monastery of Sant Esteve, founded in the 9th century and considered the 'mother monastery' of Sant Pere de Rodes *(see page 36)*. The monastery church, destroyed many times and most recently provided with a neoclassical facade, contains a fine altar by Joan Antigo (1437).

Tranquil avenue, calm waters

Also worth visiting are the 13th-century church of Santa Maria dels Turers, and several patricians' houses in the town, such as the 14th-century Casa de la Pia Almoina, which contains the **Museu Arqueològic Comarcal** (daily except Monday 10.30am–1.30pm and 4–6.30pm, Sunday 10.30am–2pm). This museum has an important collection of prehistoric finds, including the *Mandíbula de Banyoles*, the lower jaw of a Neanderthal man found near the lake in 1887; it is considered to be the oldest archaeological specimen in all Catalonia.

The old marketplace (1086) with its picturesque arcades is also definitely worth a visit; a traditional market is held there every Wednesday.

The next stop along this route is ★★ **Besalú** (pop. 2,000), impressively situated between the Riu Fluvià and the small stream known as de Capellada. The medieval town centre is full of listed buildings, and is a national monument. At least half a day can easily be spent here, taking in lots of sights: the ruined 12th-century church of Santa Maria above the town, for instance, a relic of the time when Besalú was a county (812 until the end of the 12th century) and also (briefly) even a bishopric.

The Carrer Major leads to the romantic Plaça Major with its arcades. It's not far from here to the church of **Sant Pere**. This 12th-century Romanesque church was originally part of a Benedictine monastery that was destroyed during the 19th century. One window stands out from the otherwise rather simple facade: it is framed by two lions and has ornamental pillars. Inside, the ambulatory contains some superb carving. Visible opposite the three-aisled church is the Gothic palace Casa Cornellà, which has a very attractive inner courtyard.

Romanesque Sant Pere

To the north of Sant Pere is the *mikweh* (Jewish bathhouse). Originally it was part of a synagogue built on this site in 1268 and the original building was unearthed in 2002. From the square in front of the *mikweh* there is a fine ★ view of the town's most well-known landmark, the medieval bridge (1315) over the Riu Fluvià. This old stone structure, with its watchtower at the centre, has five arches of unequal width.

Beyond Besalú is the beginning of the **Zona Volcànica de la Garrotxa**, a volcanic region created by the 40 or so volcanoes including Montasacopa, Santa Margarida and El Croscat, and today a nature reserve. Some of the most impressive scenery can be admired at ★ **Castelfollit de la Roca**. The houses of the village lie on a 60-m (196-ft) high and 1-km (½-mile) long basalt ridge, cut through by the Riu Fluvià.

57

Precipitous Castelfollit

From here it's not far to **Olot** (pop. 25,000). Though founded in the 9th century, Olot was almost completely destroyed by an earthquake in 1427, and so the historic buildings in the town centre are relatively recent: there are a few palazzi and also the church of Sant Esteve, built in 1750 on the ruins of an earlier Romanesque structure. Inside there is an altar from the school of the 'Master

Besalú on the Riu Fluvià

A lot to see in Olot

of Olot', and the small museum adjoining the church contains several fine paintings, including *Christ Bearing the Cross* by El Greco.

This university town is well worth visiting for its numerous museums. The Museu Comarcal de la Garrotxa (daily except Tuesday 11am–2pm and 4–7pm, Sunday 11am–2pm) documents local history, and is housed inside an old hospice (1777–84) in the Carrer de Hospici. There is also a small Museu d'Art Modern, housed in an annexe. The collection here features several works of the Olot School, brainchild of the painter Joaquin Vareyada i Vila (1843–94); many of the works are landscapes inspired by the volcanic scenery around the town.

There is a pleasant circular walk from the centre of Olot, leading along a marked trail through the shady Fageda d'en Jordà forest (1 hour). Another walk begins at a car park 3km (2 miles) out towards Santa Pau, taking a path leading to the Volcà Santa Margarida. At the bottom of the crater you can see a chapel next to a prehistoric *menhir*.

Sant Joan shop front

The Calvary in the church

The C-26 continues further west from Olot to Ripoll. Twelve kilometres (7½ miles) into the journey, a detour can be made to **Sant Joan de les Abadesses** (pop. 4,000). The main attraction of this little town on the banks of the Riu Ter, with its fine market-place, is the church of ★ **Sant Joan**. It was originally part of a Benedictine monastery, founded in the 9th century but then dissolved in the 19th. The single-aisled, 12th-century Romanesque church has an unusual T-shaped ground plan: the choir, ambulatory and three apsidal chapels are all situated in the main apse, but the highlight is the ★ *Calvary* on the main altar. It is a masterpiece of Romanesque wood-carving and dates from 1250. The right transept contains a Gothic altar to Maria la Blanca (the life of the Virgin is depicted here in bas-relief on 18 panels, 1443), and the 14th-century tomb of Beat Miró is also worthy of note. The entrance to the Gothic cloister (fine coffered ceiling) and cloister museum (daily 10am–2pm, 4–7pm) is to the left of the main portal.

The town of **Ripoll** (pop. 13,000) extends along the sides of a valley at the confluence of the Riu Freser and Riu Ter. Today it is an important textile and metalworking centre. During medieval times, Ripoll was where the *reconquesta* ('reconquering') of today's Catalan regions from the Moors first began. At the centre was the Benedictine **monastery of Santa Maria**, which was founded in 589. Count Guifré I had the monastery rebuilt in 888 after its destruction by the Moors. In the 11th century, under Abbot Oliba, it played a role in the foundation of the famous Monastery of Montserrat *(see page 25)*.

The monastery buildings are all at the very centre of the town, and the main architectural highlight is the monastery church's ★★ seven-arched main portal (protected by glass today to avoid damage), which has some marvellous reliefs of Biblical scenes. The rest of the church has been restored and rebuilt on several occasions over the centuries and has thus lost much stylistic unity. Inside are the tombs of Guifré, the monastery's founder, and of several other counts. The two-storey ★ cloister to the right of the portal, built between 1172 and 1509, is well-worth seeing; the capitals are very elaborately decorated. Right next to the monastery is the little 12th-century church of Sant Pere, containing the Museu Arxiu has a particularly fascinating collection of weapons; Ripoll used to be a centre of European weapon production between the 16th and 18th centuries.

The elaborate Romanesque entrance to Santa Maria

59

Beyond Ripoll, join the well-surfaced N-152 which leads northwards into the higher regions of the Pyrenees. The gradients start getting much steeper, and the views more and more impressive. From the spa resort of **Ribes de Freser** (pop. 3,000) the high peaks of the Pyrenees are already visible. A funicular railway built in the 1930s travels up to the Nuria, 13km (8 miles) away, situated beneath the highest peak in the Eastern Pyrenees, the Puigmal (2,909m/9,540ft); nearby is the picturesque mountain village of ★ **Queralbs** (1,220m/4,000ft).

Continue along the N-152 now as far as **Puigcerdà** (pop. 6,000). Picturesquely situated 1,215m (3,986ft) up in the Pyrenees, Puigcerdà is not only a holiday resort but also a transit region at the intersection of three different countries: France, Spain and Andorra. The town was founded by Alphonse I in 1177. Its 14th-century church of Santa Maria was almost completely destroyed during the Spanish Civil War; its tower and marble portal remain. The

Puigcerdà café

15th-century church of Sant Domènec was also damaged in 1938, but has since been restored; it contains some fine Gothic tapestries. The marketplace with its arcaded passageways is delightful, and there's also a very pretty lake to the north of the town.

The last 50km (30 miles) to La Seu d'Urgell provide a whole series of excellent views if the weather is fine: to the south are the 2,500-m (8,000-ft) high peaks of the Serra del Cadí, and the Cerdanya in the north is almost 3,000m (10,000ft) high. For a really spectacular evening view of the entire Cadí Massif, go to the tiny village of Lles (mountain road from Martinet).

Mansion in La Seu d'Urgell

★ **La Seu d'Urgell** (pop. 10,000) was once one of the most powerful and magnificent towns in the whole of Catalonia. It has been the seat of a bishop since the 6th century, and many magnificent buildings appeared here during the Middle Ages. Today, it is just a small market town. It gains slightly from being so close to the tax haven of Andorra. The construction of the canoeing route for the 1992 Olympics, which goes straight through the centre, hasn't exactly contributed to the town's aesthetic appeal. La Seu d'Urgell lies, half-forgotten, at the confluence of the Riu Segre and the Riu Valira.

The Old Town, however, contains a magnificent monument to its former glory: the **Cathedral of Santa Maria**. This three-aisled building was begun in 1116 under the supervision of a Lombard architect who added several Italian elements, e.g. the narrow gallery with its double columns on the outer facade of the central apse in the transept. The two towers, apparently unfinished, are also worthy of note: they start off square and end up octagonal, and are no higher than the cathedral itself.

The basilica, 38m (124ft) long and 21m (68ft) wide, is entered via the main portal, which is decorated with figures of men and lions. The interior is rather simple (much of the art was destroyed during the Spanish Civil War). The central apse contains a Romanesque statue of the Virgin Mary, and the original frescoes are now housed in the Museu d'Art de Catalunya in Barcelona.

Cathedral cloister
Museu Diocesà: the Apocalypse

The 13th-century Romanesque cloister borders the cathedral to the south; it contains 50 granite capitals, some of them very richly decorated, and can be entered via the Museu Diocesà (Diocesan Museum: June to October 10am–1pm and 4–7pm, otherwise Saturday and Sunday only 10am–1pm). The latter contains frescoes, altarpieces, and several Romanesque and Gothic artefacts including a 10th-century *Apocalypse* by Beatus of Liébana. The 11th-century church of San Miquel, with its impressive frescoes, also forms part of the museum.

Route 8

Andorra

La Seu d'Urgell – Andorra La Vella – Port d'Envalirà
(60km/37 miles) *See map on pages 54–5*

The magnificent mountain scenery in the principality of Andorra is certainly worth a visit, even for those primarily interested in the beaches of the Costa Brava. The wild mountain streams, deep ravines and snow-capped peaks in the region are highly romantic. The capital, Andorra La Vella, is also a shoppers' paradise, thanks to the country's liberal tax laws.

This small state has a surface area of 462sq km (178sq miles), and a population of 49,000. The lowest point of Andorra is 840m (2,755ft) above sea-level, the highest is the Pic de Bareites (2,951m/9,681ft).

Legend has it that Charlemagne granted the area a charter of liberties in AD784. Andorra received its first historical mention in the consecration document of the cathedral in La Seu d'Urgell in 839, where it is listed as forming part of the county of Urgell. In 1133 the Count of Urgell made a present of it to the bishop. Andorra's dual allegiance to two princes, one French and one Spanish, originated in an argument during the late 13th century between the Spanish bishops of Urgell and the French heirs to the countship. In 1278 the *pareatges*, a document that made the dual allegiance official, was signed, and Andorra is run to this day by two 'coprinces': the bishop of La Seu d'Urgell and the French president.

Andorra has had a government since 1419. The supreme administrative body in Andorra itself is the elected Council

61

Andorra's Les Escaldes

Policing the shopping crowds

General of the Valleys. All legislative, executive and judicial powers are granted to permanent delegates or judges, known as *viguirs*. The male population was given the right to vote in 1933; the women only joined them as recently as 1970. There are two official languages, French and Catalan.

Since the 1950s, Andorra has been a free-trade zone without any taxes or customs duties, and this has radically altered everyday life: the whole country has come to resemble one enormous supermarket, there are queues of cars at all of its numerous filling stations, and most visitors only stay long enough to stock up on food and drink before leaving again. Tourism is also an important source of income. The valleys and mountains are ideal for hiking, climbing, fishing and every kind of winter sport. Numerous thermal baths, including the beautiful La Caldea Roman baths in the capital, and six enormous winter sports centres with 17 chairlifts and over 40 ski-lifts await hundreds of thousands of visitors all year round.

Just beyond the border post is **Sant Julià de Lória** (pop. 6,000). This rather modern town has a Romanesque church, containing an interesting 17th-century crucifix. The chapel of ★ **Sant Serni** in nearby Nagol (2km/1 mile to the northwest, consecrated in 1055) with its Early Romanesque frescoes is definitely worth a visit.

A few kilometres beyond Sant Julià, the Romanesque bridge of La Margineda leads across the Riu Gran Valira. Shortly afterwards, the town of **Santa Coloma** comes into view with its Early Romanesque church. It has a round, five-storeyed tower, double windows and a round pointed roof; inside there is a 12th-century statue of the Virgin. Above the town, the restored ruins of the 12th-century Castell de Sant Vicenç can be made out.

La Caldea roman baths

The next stop is **Andorra la Vella** (pop. 18,000), the capital of Andorra. This busy town, with its many banks and souvenir shops, lies at the foot of the Puig d'Enclar (2,317m/7,600ft). An interesting sight here is the **Casa de la Vall** ('House of the Valleys'), the seat of the Council General since 1580. The building has a big square tower with a pyramid roof. Access to it is through a portal bearing the coats-of-arms of the various municipalities of Andorra, and sights inside include the kitchen, the Capella Sant Ermengol on the first floor, and the Salle de Conseil (council chamber) itself. A cupboard, originally secured by six locks (by seven since 1978), contains the Archive of Andorra. Another good place to visit in Andorra la Vella is the church of Sant Esteve, with its Romanesque apse.

Casa de la Vall

The N-2 leads northeastwards now from Andorra la Vella, past the confluence of the Riu Valira del Nord and the Riu Valira d'Orient. The road up to Port d'Envalira is worth following just for the landscape alone; the tiny Romanesque village churches are also highly picturesque. In **Escaldes-Engordany** you can enjoy a splash in the ★ **Caldea hot springs**. To the north of the town is the 12th-century **Capella de Sant Miquel d' Engolasters**, with some attractive frescoes inside. Further on, in **Encamp** (pop. 6,000), is the 12th-century church of Santa Eulalia, and a short way out of the town in the direction of Canillo, the delightful little 12th-century chapel of **Les Bons** with its fine retable and frescoes.

63

Capella de Sant Miquel de Engolasters

Three kilometres (1½ miles) before Canillo, a road branches off in the direction of the **Santuari Meritxell**. This shrine to the local patron saint is the most important place of pilgrimage in Andorra, and is packed with people on 8 September each year. The old chapel was destroyed by fire in 1972, but the Catalan architect Ricardo Bofill has created a new building above the ruins; its dark colour harmonises well with the surrounding scenery. At the centre of the complex there is a wooden copy of the Holy Virgin of Meritxell.

Canillo (pop. 1,500) is the last community the road passes through before it starts to wind its way up the steep mountains. A short distance outside the town is the Romanesque chapel of Sant Joan de Caselles (10th–12th centuries). It contains an altarpiece dating from 1525 and also a fresco of the Crucifixion (unfortunately damaged). Beyond Canillo the road starts twisting uphill towards the **Porta d'Envalira**, a mountain pass that reaches a maximum elevation of 2,407m (7,896ft). The road is well-surfaced (it cannot be used between December and April, however, because of bad weather), and leads travellers straight into France.

Snow melts into the mountain streams

Route 9

The Heights of the Pyrenees

La Seu d'Urgell – Sort – Val d'Aran – Vielha (127km/78 miles) *See map on pages 54–5*

The magnificent Val d'Aran, 1,000m (3,280ft) above sea level, was almost inaccessible until just a few years ago. Today there are numerous skiing areas here, and lots of hiking trails leading down into lonely valleys and up to stunning views. Tiny Romanesque churches keep appearing along this route, nestling beneath the enormous peaks of the Pyrenees. It's worth devoting at least a day to this tour.

Val d'Aran villagers

Leave La Seu d'Urgell along the N-260 in a southerly direction and follow it further westwards at Adrall. The road now winds its way along a 30-km (18-mile) long stretch of road as far as **Sort** (pop. 1,500), romantically situated in the valley of the Riu Noguera Pallaresa. There aren't many historic sights to see here apart from the ruins of the 6th-century castle that once belonged to the counts of Pallars, but the stunning landscape more than makes up for that. River-rafting can be organised here, as can hanggliding and horseback-riding. Twelve kilometres (7½ miles) to the west of the town is the skiing area of Llessiu, with its three enormous lifts and 21 *pistes*.

Approaching the valley from La Seu d'Urgell

Leave Sort now and carry on northwards through the Noguera Valley. There are several attractive little villages along the river. Just before Llavorsi a road branches off to the right and makes quite a good detour (40km/25 miles there and back) to the valleys of two rivers, the Riu Noguera de Vall de Ferrera and the Riu Noguera de Cardós.

Back on the C-13, the next stop on the route is **La Guingueta** (pop. 55), which is not so much a village as a collection of houses, idyllically situated on the shore of the Torrasa Reservoir. This is such an atmospheric place that everyone should take at least a short break here before moving on. The nearby village of **Esterri d'Aneu** (pop. 600) is famed for its Romanesque church of Santa Maria. Several 11th-century frescoes by the Master of Pedret were discovered here and are now on display in Barcelona's Museu d'Art de Catalunya.

From Esterri, a bumpy track leads 13km (8 miles) to **Espot** (pop. 300). This village is the starting-point for hikes to the nearby ★★ **national park of Aigüestortes i Estany Sant Maurici**, with its romantic valleys, pine forests, mountain streams and lakes – all of them surrounded by

Autumn in Aigüestortes

magnificent 3,000m- (10,000-ft) high mountains. It's worth spending at least two days in this region.

The pass known as the ★ **Port de la Bonaigua** (closed between November and April) is an equally memorable experience. After a series of seemingly endless hairpins, the road reaches an altitude of 2,000m (6,560ft) here. Roughly halfway up, there is a small restaurant next to a stream – a perfect place for a break. At the top it's worth braving the cold for the superb 360° view of the ★★ **Val d'Aran**. The valley covers an area of 600sq km (231sq miles) from west to east, and is protected on its northern and southern flanks by high mountains, including the Maladeta Massif towering to the south-west, whose **Pico de Aneto** (3,404m/11,168ft) is the highest mountain in the Pyrenees. The valley's inhabitants live off dairy farming and forestry. Their language is not pure Catalan, but a dialect strongly influenced by French, known as *Aranès*.

The next stop is **Salardú** (pop. 300), not only a winter sports centre but also an important cultural site. The village was fortified in the Middle Ages (parts of the wall still survive), and it contains an architectural jewel: the church of **Sant Andreu**. Built in the transitional style between Romanesque and Gothic, the church has a simple yet beautiful entrance portal (four archivolts). The main apse inside contains the majestic 13th-century crucifix sculpture known as the *Christ of Salardú*.

Salardú, with the Maladeta in the background

The next village on the route, **Arties** (pop. 400), also has a fine 12th-century church, Sant Joan, The adjoining museum is definitely worth a visit, as is the 13th-century church of Santa Maria, which contains an altar painting by the Master of Ax (15th century). There is also a fine 13th-century font with interesting bas-reliefs.

Vielha (pop. 2,000) is the capital of the Val d'Aran. The fantastic mountain scenery around here (peaks between 900m/3,000ft and 1,800m/6,000ft) is perfect for walking and hiking holidays. Sights in the town include the little market-place and also the 12th-century church of **Sant Miquel**. This single-aisled church, built on a cruciform ground-plan, has an octagonal 16th-century bell-tower and an imposing entrance portal with four archivolts. Inside, there is an elaborately-carved 15th-century Gothic altar, and also, in a side chapel, the *Christ of Mijaran*, a 12th-century figure of Christ that once formed part of a larger *Deposition*. The **Museu Etnológico de Vielha** (Tuesday to Saturday 10am–1pm and 5–8pm, Sunday 10am–2pm) is housed inside the Tor Deth Generau Martinhon in the Carrer Major. It contains an interesting collection of medieval tools, textiles and furniture.

Nature's heartlands
Sant Miquel: altar detail

Route 10

The Romanesque Road

Vielha – Pont de Suert – (Vall de Boi) – Tremp – Lleida (184km/114 miles) *See map on pages 54–5*

The road to Lleida

This route from the Val d'Aran to the provincial capital of Lleida is not for those in a hurry. Lovers of Romanesque architecture and stunning landscape will find it hard to forget the wonderful churches along the Riu Noguera de Tort (Boí Valley) and also Tremp and Balaguer, before arriving at the fascinating town of Lleida. Because of the lengthy mountain drives along this route, an overnight stay (e.g. in Tremp) is highly advisable.

Leave the Val d'Aran to the south on the N-230. Go through the Vielha Tunnel (built in 1948, 6km/4 miles long) to reach the south side of the Pyrenees. The landscape starts getting gentler again. Roughly 3km (1¾ miles) before the little town of Pont de Suert, a country road branches off northeastwards. This 30-km (18-mile) stretch of road goes through the Vall de Boí, where Christians hid from persecution during the Middle Ages and built some magnificent churches. The latter were subsidised by the wealthy counts of Toulouse and also the barons of Erill, who had made a name for themselves – and a lot of money – fighting the Moors (1118).

The churches in the ★ **Vall de Boí** are quite magnificent. The little church of Santa Maria in **Coll** has a lower tower than the other ones in the valley. The apse of the single-aisled building has several Lombard elements. **Barruera**, the administrative centre of the valley, contains the church of Sant Feliu with its three apses and bell-tower.

This town is a good starting-point for hikes into the nearby **national park of Aigüestortes** *(see page 64)*. **Durro** is just off the main road, and also has a fine 12th-century Romanesque church, the Esglesia Nativitat de la Mare de Deu. But the most famous examples of Romanesque architecture can be discovered in the region around **Boí**.

In ★★ **Taüll**, two structures catch the eye. The first is the church of **Sant Climent** up on the hillside, with its seemingly oversized six-storey bell-tower. The church was consecrated in 1123, and contains several striking frescoes. The *Pantocrator* here is world-famous. The second church is Santa Maria (1123) with its five-storey campanile. The originals of the frescoes here are on display in the Museu d'Art de Catalunya in Barcelona. The village of **Erill-la-Vall** is a few kilometres away in the western part of the valley. Its 13th-century church of Santa

Sant Climent de Taüll's lofty tower and the famous fresco

Eulàlia, with its narrow campanile, is definitely worth a visit. By way of contrast, **Caldes de Boí** doesn't have any historical sights to speak of, but it's a famous spa town; there are 37 thermal springs here.

Further along the route, the striking-looking modern church at the centre of **Pont de Suert** (pop. 3,000) was built in 1955 by Torroja and Rodríguez Mijares. For motorists, the next 40km (24 miles) of this route require more concentration than anything so far: the road climbs to an altitude of 1,300m (4,250ft) and more, crosses the Coll de Perves, and then arrives at the town of **La Pobla de Segur** (pop. 3,500). It is situated on the northern edge of the enormous Sant Antoni Reservoir, and is a good starting-point for tours of the Pyrenees. There's also some good fishing to be had here.

Olive mill, La Pobla de Segur and the mountains nearby

The route now continues along the reservoir for almost 16km (10 miles) as far as **Tremp** (pop. 5,000). The giant power station near this small industrial town utilises the Riu Noguera Pallasera to generate hydro-electricity. Tremp has a small old section, with the ruins of a medieval town wall.

Harnessing the mountain rivers

The section of the route between Tremp and Balaguer passes three reservoirs: Dels Terradets, De Camerasa and De Sant Llorenç. Beyond Cellers the C-13 winds its way through a narrow angle created by the mountain ranges of Montsec d'Ares to the west and Montsec de Rùbies to the east.

The attractive town of **Balaguer** (pop. 13,000) on the banks of the Riu Segre has one of the largest market squares in the country (Plaça del Mercadal), and its main source of income is fruit cultivation. Founded in the 9th century, Balaguer became the administrative centre of the county of Urgell in 1106. The church of Santa Maria, with its striking octagonal tower and clock, dates from this prosperous period. It was consecrated in 1575 and various additions were made during the centuries that followed. Visit the Romanesque church of Sant Salvador and the baroque church of Sant Crist – and don't miss a visit to the Monastery of Sant Domènec. Its 14th-century Gothic cloister, with its slender columns, conveys a marvellous architectural lightness. Castell Formós, the former palace of the counts of Urgell, has yielded several archaeological finds dating from Moorish times, and they can be admired in the Museu Comarcal in the Plaza del Comptes d'Urgell, 5 (Tuesday to Friday 11am–2pm and 6.30–8.30pm, Saturday and Sunday 11am–2pm).

A trip into the mountains is a very good idea at this stage. Take the C-12 northwestwards from Balaguer across the Port d'Ager pass (903m/2,960ft) and visit the picturesque village of Ager (distance there and back 66km/41 miles). On the way, a stopover in Bellpuig de les Avellanes is recommended. The **Monastery of Santa Maria** there was founded by a count of Urgell in 1166. It was extended later by Count Ermengol X, who had tombs erected for himself and his family in the Gothic church. Sections of the old 12th-century Romanesque cloister can still be seen, as can the ruins of the never-completed Gothic church (14th century). Other highlights include the dormitory, kitchen and chapter house of the Premonstratensian Order.

Lleida

★ ★ **Lleida** (pop. 100,000) lies in a low plain on the edge of the Riu Segre and is known as *Lérida* in Castilian. Four bridges, the oldest of which is the Pont Vell, connect the older parts of the city in the north with the newer sections to the south. High on a hill above the old part of the city is the cathedral, in a strategically favourable location and looking more like a castle; it's not surprising that it was used for many years as a military barracks. The city is also an important traffic junction.

Lleida's Old Cathedral

Lleida dates back to an early Celtic settlement. The Romans and the Visigoths were followed in the 8th century by the Moors, who were driven out in turn by Count Ramón Berenguer IV in 1149. The town experienced its heyday during this period, and was granted the first royal university in 1300, during the reign of Jaume II. At the beginning of the 18th century, like many other towns in Catalonia, it was occupied by French troops during the Spanish War of Succession and several parts of it were seriously damaged. The Spanish Civil War during the 20th century also resulted in the destruction of sections of the Old Town.

The tour begins in the northwestern part of the Old Town on the **Plaça Sant Llorenç**. The church of **Sant Llorenç** on this square was built on the site of a Moorish mosque in 13th century, and its architecture represents the transition from Romanesque to Gothic. There is a striking octagonal bell-tower, 76m (250ft) high. The interior of the three-aisled church contains four very impressive altar reliefs dating from the 14th century. The *retable of Santa Ursula*, depicting scenes from the life of the saint, is also particularly fine.

Inside the New Cathedral

Leave the church now and walk down the Carrer dels Descalços and the Carrer de les Carmelites to the **Plaça de la Catedral**. On the northern side of this square is the neoclassical **Catedral Nova**, a rather austere and not very popular place. Built between 1761 and 1792, it was severely damaged during the Civil War. On the opposite side of the square, the ★ **Hospital de Santa Maria** (15th century), has a delightful inner courtyard with slender arcades. It contains a small archaeological museum and also the town archives.

Hospital de Santa Maria

From the cathedral square, the long Carrer Major leads into the ever-narrower streets of the Old Town. After a five minutes' walk, the **Casa de la Paeria** (Town Hall) appears on the right. It dates from the 13th century, and has some well-preserved Romanesque sections (the courtyard), though the facade is far more recent (1868). A few yards further on the only surviving town gate, the **Arco del Puente**, leads to the Pont Vell bridge.

Continue along the Carrer Major to the imposing-looking Plaça de Sant Joan. An elevator leads from here up to the mighty **Old Cathedral** (La Seu Vella), which dominates the square. It was consecrated in 1278, though construction work continued until well into the 14th century.

The Porta de Sant Berenguer on the north side leads into the imposing three-aisled basilica with its five apses. Only a handful of the 27 chapels here are in any kind of reasonable condition, but the two south portals (Porta de la Anunciación, Porta dels Fillols), both built in around 1215, with their marvellous leaf motifs, form an impressive contrast. Unfortunately, the cathedral was used as a barracks from 1707 to 1947, and is today certainly the worst maintained of all the large cathedrals in Catalonia. However, just how magnificent the cathedral once was can be appreciated from the southern part of the 14th-century ★ **cloister**, which has a marvellous windowed gallery with a fine view across the city. The 60-m (195-ft) high tower adjoining the cloister also faces the town.

The cloister has grand views

69

Just a few minutes' walk away from the Old Cathedral is the Romanesque church of **Sant Martí**, which was formerly the university chapel. Today it contains a fascinating exhibition of 12th- and 13th-century sculpture.

Outside Hospital de Santa Maria

Catalan countryman

Route 11

Provincial Charm

Barcelona – Vic – Berga – La Seu d'Urgell – Organyà – Solsona – Manresa – Barcelona (364km/226 miles)
See map on pages 54–5

Away from Barcelona and its popular coastline, Catalonia is a far sleepier place. This round trip from Barcelona goes through the provincial, agricultural region at the centre of Catalonia and provides a fascinating assortment of landscapes. The trip takes between two and four days to complete, and includes leafy forest regions such as the Serra de Montseny as well as the Cadí-Moixeró National Park in the Pyrenees. Art lovers will adore the episcopal museum in Vic with its famous Romanesque collection, as well as the various castles along the route.

Leave Barcelona on the E-15 in the direction of Girona, and roughly 10km (6 miles) later turn north onto the C-17 (which at this point very much resembles a motorway). On the right now is **Granollers** (pop. 40,000). This little town is rapidly becoming a major industrial centre thanks to its proximity to Barcelona. The region here has always been very fertile, as evidenced by the town's former Corn Exchange *(Porxada)*, which dates from the 16th century; the buildings around the Plaça Gran (16th- and 17th-century, also art nouveau) are also worthy of note, though perhaps not worth a proper detour off the C-17.

Beyond Granollers the road gradually starts to climb, and passes the spa towns of La Garriga and Tona, both of them very popular weekend destinations with the people of Barcelona. It's possible to take a short detour from

Landscape near Berga

Tona to the ★ **Serra de Montseny** (Tona–Montseny over-all return distance 52km/32 miles). This marvellous mountain region with its forests, small farms, hamlets and marked routes is perfect for hikers. The mountains here are around 1,700m (5,600ft) high (Turó de l'Home 1,712m/5,616ft), and every few moments there's a new and breathtaking view to be had.

The rural town of ★ **Vic** (pop. 30,000), also the seat of an archbishop, dates back to an Iberian settlement which was known to the Romans as *Ausa* (the Old Town contains a restored Temple of Diana dating from that period), and from the 10th century onwards it was the seat of the Counts of Ausona. The triple-aisled cathedral with its three-storey cloisters is definitely worth a visit. Construction work began on it in the 11th century under Abbot Oliba from the nearby monastery in Ripoll. The cathedral was seriously damaged on several occasions over the centuries, and in 1803 it was rebuilt in neoclassical style. The 46-m (150-ft) high, six-storeyed Romanesque bell-tower is most impressive. Inside the church, one is struck immediately by the massive frescoes in the side-chapels and in the main apse. They are the work of Josep Maria Sert (1874–1945), a Catalan artist who worked here for many years. Also worthy of note are the Gothic alabaster altar by Pere Ollers (1427) and the baroque silver coffin for Bishop Bernat Calbó (died 1423). The three-storeyed Gothic cloister is dominated by the huge tomb of the philosopher and mathematician Jaume Balmes (1810–48), who was born in Vic.

Vic's bell-tower

71

Next to the cathedral is the ★★ **Episcopal Museum** (winter: Tuesday to Friday 10am–1pm and 3–6pm, Saturday 10am–7pm, Sunday 10am–2pm; summer: Tuesday to Saturday 10am–7pm, Sunday 10am–2pm), which contains the second-best collection of Romanesque art in all Catalonia (the Museu d'Art de Catalunya in Barcelona being the most comprehensive). There is a large collection of Romanesque frescoes here, many of them from the surrounding area. The museum also has good Gothic, baroque and prehistoric sections.

A calm corner of Berga

The market town of **Berga** (pop. 14,000) is surrounded by mountains over 2,000m (6,500ft) high. Textile processing has played a major role here ever since Roman times, and a new spinning machine, the 'Berguedana', was invented here in the 18th century. The surrounding area is very attractive, ideal for hiking, hunting and fishing, and for nearly every type of winter sport.

Those keen on history should visit the basilica of San Quirze de Pedret (4km/2½ miles east of Berga). The church has some Pre-Romanesque sections; it was here that the frescoes by the 'Master of Pedret' were found. They are

At home in the provinces

Reservoir near Organyà

Virgen del Claustre, Solsona

now on display in Barcelona (Museu d'Art de Catalunya) and Solsona *(see below)*. The pilgrimage church of Nuestra Señora de Queralt is 4km (2½ miles) to the west of Berga, and contains a 14th-century statue of the Virgin. The hotel next to it affords a fine view of the mountains.

Beyond Berga the route follows the shore of the La Baells Reservoir, passes through the communities of Guardiola de Berguedà and Baga *(see below)* and then enters the 5-km (3-mile) long Túnel del Cadí (tunnel toll). At the other end, cross the flat, fertile plain to reach La Seu d'Urgell *(see page 60)*. There's a worthwhile detour at this point, however, to the nature reserve of **Cadí-Moixeró**, 30km (18 miles) north of Berga. The limestone massif with its strange rock formation contains a whole network of marked hiking routes. The best starting-point for any trip into this region is the little village of **Baga** (on the C-16).

For the return trip to Barcelona, take the N260 and then C-14 through the attractive Segre Valley and then into the Organyà Gorge (Gorje de Organyà). At the end of it is the little town of **Organyà** (pop. 1,100). In the market-place, a round building stands as a memorial to the fact that the oldest ever manuscript written in Catalan, the so-called *Homilies d'Organyà*, dating from the late 12th century, was found in the nearby church of Santa Maria.

Just beyond Organyà is another reservoir framed by massive mountains; up on a small rise to the right, the picturesque village of Coll de Nargó comes into view, with its 11th-century Romanesque church of Sant Climent.

In Bassella, leave the C-14 and carry on eastwards along the C-26. **Solsona** (pop. 7,000) has a particularly fine old section, situated at the foot of the rise known as Castellvell (with a ruined castle at the top); the ancient walls are still partially intact. A gate provides access to the Old Town, and to the cathedral. The three apses and the bell-tower are Romanesque (1070), the nave is of Gothic origin, and the facade is baroque. Inside, the 12th-century statue of the **Virgen del Claustre**, the town's patron saint, can be seen on the high altar.

The 18th-century episcopal palace houses the **Diocesan Museum** (Tuesday to Saturday 10am–1pm and 4.30–7pm in summer; 10am–1pm and 4–6pm in winter, Sunday 10am–2pm), which was opened in 1896. It contains not only several fascinating archaeological finds but also numerous Romanesque works of art discovered in the 100 or so medieval churches and chapels in the vicinity. Sculptures and altar paintings, some by the 15th-century artists Lluís Borrassà and Jaume Ferrer, can be admired alongside frescoes from Sant Quirce de Pedret and Sant Pau de Casserres. One particularly fine fresco, known as *Orant*

('Worshipper'), was painted in the 10th century and is possibly the oldest Christian fresco in Catalonia. The first room in the museum is dedicated to salt and shows how important the region between Solsona and Manresa has been for the salt trade ever since Roman times. There are also some impressive salt sculptures on exhibit.

The route now crosses a flat section of landscape with numerous olive groves before arriving at ★ **Cardona** (pop. 6,000). This town lies below a medieval fortress that was originally built as a defence against the Moors; it was later extended, and served for many years as a military barracks. Today it is a state-run *Parador* hotel, and the view from up here of the salt-mining region below is superb. The church of Sant Vicenç is also worth a visit; like the cathedral in La Seu d'Urgell it was built between 1029 and 1040 by Lombard architects, and thus has many Italianate stylistic features. The narrow, three-aisled structure has just a hint of a transept, and three apses. Inside there are several Gothic frescoes, including one of St Ursula.

St Ursula in Cardona and Solsona's Salt Museum

73

Cardona and its fortress

Manresa (pop. 60,000) is an industrial centre today, but it can look back over a long history. The Romans knew it as *Munorisa*, and during the Middle Ages it was the capital of an autonomous county. The most striking historical structure here is the basilica of Santa Maria de la Seu, situated up on a hill. This mighty Gothic church with its eye-catching square bell-tower (1592) was built between 1328 and 1548. Inside, the highlight is a retable by Pere Serra (1394), depicting episodes in the life of Christ.

Ignatius of Loyola (1491–1556), the founder of the Jesuit Order, is meant to have spent some time in Manresa and engaged in spiritual exercises here. He spent up to seven hours a day in prayer in the Santa Cova ('holy cave') next to the baroque Jesuit church (1760). The town became famous for quite another reason at the end of the 19th

Soaking up the sunshine

century, however. In the Casa de la Ciutat here in 1892, the *Bases de Manresa* were established by the Unió Catalanista, an assembly of nationalist groups; they were to form the basis for the constitution of Catalonia.

Just 5km (3 miles) north of Manresa is the monastery of **Sant Benet de Bages**. First mentioned in 960, this monastery was almost completely destroyed by the Moors in 1125, but was then rebuilt almost immediately. The Romanesque church with its three apses dates from this time. The 13th-century cloister contains beautifully decorated capitals; some of the motifs date from the period before the destruction of the monastery (e.g. three 10th-century bas-reliefs depicting a beardless *Christ*, a *Priest*, and the *Annunciation*). The monastery was modernised by the architect Puig i Cadafalch *(see page 85);* today it is privately-owned, and provides a haven of rest and relaxation from the hectic pace of the nearby industrial town.

South of Manresa on the C-16 is **Terrassa** (pop. 150,000). This fast-growing town, which started life in Roman times as *Egara*, has a particularly successful textiles industry, but it's certainly worth visiting for its ★ **churches**. The Sant Pere d'Egara section of town has a fine collection of sacred buildings all bunched together in the early Christian manner: episcopal basilica, baptistery and church (all open Tuesday to Saturday 10am–1.30pm and 4–7pm, Sunday 11am–2pm).

The church of Sant Miquel (5th–9th century) is the oldest of the three structures. It dates from Visigothic and Carolingian times, as can be seen from the building materials used (layers of brick between squared stonework), the dome and also the ground-plan, which is in the shape of a Greek cross. The interior contains Carolingian frescoes and an underground crypt; there is also a Gothic altar by Jaume Cirera and Guillem Talarn. The basilica of Santa Maria dates from the 12th century (parts of it are even earlier). Beneath a picture of Christ in one of the side-apses, a fresco depicts the murder in 1170 of Thomas Becket, Archbishop of Canterbury. There is also a fine altar (1460) by Jaume Huguet. The church of Sant Pere has a Visigothic transept and choir; the nave was built somewhat later (12th century). The architraves here with their statues of saints, separating the nave from the transepts, are particularly striking. The church also contains a magnificent altar by Lluís Borrassà (1413).

The **Museu Téxtil Biosca** (Tuesday to Friday 9am–6pm, Thursday 9am–9pm) is situated in the Parc de Vallparadis. It contains a fine collection of textiles and materials of Old Spanish and Moorish origin, and also embroidery and textile products from nearly everywhere in the world.

From Terrassa the C-16 motorway leads back via Sabadell to Barcelona.

Route 12

Catalonia's Cistercian Monasteries

**Tarragona – Valls – Santes Creus – Poblet – Lleida
(132km/82 miles)** *See map on page 76*

There are two magnificent Cistercian monasteries inland
from the Costa Daurada. Both are fine examples of the Cistercian architectural style, which was imported from
France and introduced the Gothic style to Catalonia. The
final destination on this route – which can be done in a day
if properly planned – is the provincial capital of Lleida,
which is a good place to spend the night.

The first stop on the N-240 is **Valls** (pop. 18,000). This
town has a fine old section, with the remains of a medieval
town wall and a former Jewish Quarter. The 16th-century church of **Sant Joan** (neo-Gothic bell-tower) contains
the Capilla de Nuestra Senyora del Roser. This chapel
houses a magnificent depiction, on painted tiles, of the
Christian defeat of the Turks at the Battle of Lepanto
(1571). Valls is also thought to have originated the not
entirely safe custom of *castells*, or human pyramids *(see
page 86)*. The acrobatics can be admired here in June during the festival of Sant Joan.

*Valls: Sant Joan's tower
and a tiled shop front*

Continue eastwards from Valls along the C-51 in the
direction of El Vendrell. After 10km (6 miles), turn off
northwards in the direction of El Pont d'Armentera and
5km (3 miles) further on the ★ **Monestir Santes Creus**
(April to October 10am–1.30pm and 3–7pm, November
to March 10am–1.30pm and 3–5.30pm) comes into view,
magnificently situated in the valley of the Riu Gaià. It was
founded in the mid-12th century, during the reign of Count

Monestir Santes Creus

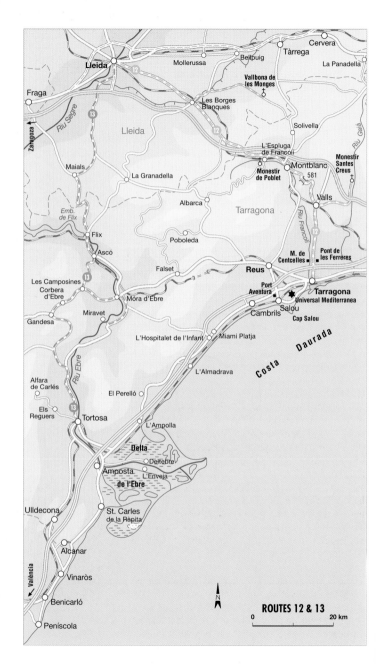

ROUTES 12 & 13

0   20 km

Ramón Berenguer IV, and then run by monks from Southern France. In the centuries that followed it became more and more of a fortress, and was also selected as the last resting-place of the kings of Aragón. Architecturally, this 'monastery of the Holy Cross' represents the transition between the Romanesque and Gothic styles. After secularisation in 1835 it was ransacked and partially destroyed, but the restoration work has been exemplary.

The monastery is entered through a simple portal, leading into a courtyard containing the Capilla de Santa Llúcia (1741). A second portal leads on to the **Plaça Major** with its baroque fountain for Abbot Bernhard and the **Abbots' Residence**. Straight ahead is the Romanesque portal of the **monastery church**, which was begun in the Romanesque style in 1174 but then continued in the far stricter Cistercian manner until its consecration in 1211. The ground-plan is in the form of a Latin cross, with five square apsidal chapels, and the choir is closed off by a straight wall. Massive cruciform pillars separate the 21-m (68-ft) high central aisle from the 10-m (32-ft) high side-aisles. Just before the crossing with its octagonal dome, the tombs of King Pere III (1276–85) and Jaume II (1285–1327) can be seen below some ornamental baldachins; Jaume II is resting beside his wife, Blanche de Anjou (the daughter of Charles II of Naples).

Portal into Plaça Major and column detail

Outside, to the right of the church, is the entrance to the monastery proper. It leads firstly to the **New Cloister** (1313–41) with its playfully carved capitals in the Late Gothic Flamboyant style. The small round structure with the fountain is probably Romanesque. The eastern side of the cloister gives access to the almost square, three-aisled **chapter house**, supported by four 14th-century pillars, and with the tombs of several former abbots set into its pavement. A flight of steps leads to the upper floor and to the monks' dormitory, almost 46m (150ft) long and supported by 11 pointed arches. The **Old Cloister** was built in 1153 and is astonishingly simple, with hardly a trace of ornamentation; the pointed arches are very low. This cloister is surrounded by the former wine cellar, the kitchen, the refectory and the remains of the Royal Palace with its pretty courtyard.

The Old Cloister dates from 1153

Those in a hurry can take the E-90 motorway from the monastery to Montblanc, the next stop on the route. For some superb landscape, however, drive back to Valls and then head north on the N-240. Roughly 10km (6 miles) outside the town the road winds its way up to the pass known as Coll de L'Illa (581m/1,906ft). From the Mirador del Camp de Tarragona restaurant and the Parador hotel above it there is a fantastic ★ view, stretching as far as Tarragona and the sea beyond.

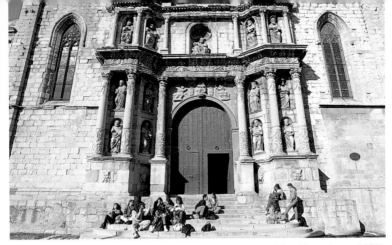

Montblanc's Santa Maria church

The Visigothic bridge

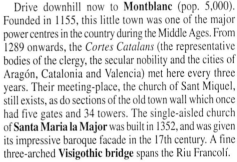
Monastery of Santa Maria de
Poblet: Porta Daurada

Drive downhill now to **Montblanc** (pop. 5,000). Founded in 1155, this little town was one of the major power centres in the country during the Middle Ages. From 1289 onwards, the *Cortes Catalans* (the representative bodies of the clergy, the secular nobility and the cities of Aragón, Catalonia and Valencia) met here every three years. Their meeting-place, the church of Sant Miquel, still exists, as do sections of the old town wall which once had five gates and 34 towers. The single-aisled church of **Santa Maria la Major** was built in 1352, and was given its impressive baroque facade in the 17th century. A fine three-arched **Visigothic bridge** spans the Riu Francolí.

Turn off the main road 6km (3 miles) beyond Montblanc and head for L'Espluga de Francolí. From there it's just another 4km (2½ miles) to the ★★ **Monastery of Santa Maria de Poblet** (daily October to March 10am–12.30pm and 3–5.30pm, March to October 11am–12.30pm and 3–6pm). Set in green landscape and surrounded by its 1.8-km (1-mile) long wall, this complex of buildings is more reminiscent of a secular royal residence than a monastic refuge. The Cistercian monastery was founded by Count Ramón Berenguer IV in 1150, before being entrusted (like Santes Creus) to monks from Southern France. During the 13th and 14th centuries the monastery received substantial royal patronage, and for many years Poblet was probably the most important spiritual centre in Catalonia. It was ransacked in 1835, but since then has been rebuilt – and since 1940 has actually been run by monks again.

The massive **Porta Daurada** (1493) with its towers forms the entrance to the large courtyard of the Plaça Major. Behind it on the left is the little Romanesque chapel of Santa Catalina (1251). On the eastern side of this square on the left is the Porta Reial. This simple but very imposing entrance gate to the monastery area was built between 1379 and 1397. The church portal (1670) on the right, set into the sturdy-looking defensive wall, is of baroque origin; it has figures of St Bernard and St Benedict, with the Virgin above them. Go through the Porta Reial now and enter the monastery proper. On the other side of the gate is an antechamber with a staircase leading up to the right to the monastery museum (sculpture, altarpieces, goldsmiths' work). This museum is housed above the west wing of the cloister, in the rooms of the Late Gothic Palau de Sant Martí (14th-century) which was never completed. The magnificent 13th-century cloister with its fountain pavilion is surrounded by the old wine cellar, the restored kitchen, the refectory and the library, which is built in the style of a pillared basilica. Next to it is the chapter house with its fine ribbed vault.

The monastery church can either be entered via the cloister or via the main portal as described above. It was built between 1170 and the 14th century, and its garland of chapels in the ambulatory is not typical of Cistercian architecture by any means. The striking alabaster high altar in the apse of this three-aisled basilica, by the sculptor Damián Forment (1460–1540), shows *Scenes from the life of Christ* in four series of bas-reliefs, with a *Crucifixion* above. Also very impressive are the **tombs of the kings of Aragón**, restored quite recently by the contemporary sculptor Frederic Marés. The right-hand side-aisle of the basilica gives access to the baroque New Sacristy (1732–36), with its marvellous frescoed dome (18th-century) by José Bernard Flaugier. A flight of steps off the left-hand side-aisle leads to the 87-m (285-ft) long monks' dormitory with its 19 pointed arches.

Leave Poblet now and follow the N-240 northwards to **Les Borges Blanques** (pop. 500). This tiny town is the centre of olive oil production in Catalonia. Groves of olives and almonds extend for miles around, irrigated by water from the Canal d'Urgell. In the town itself, the Parc del Terrall contains an oil press monument, and a 17th-century oil mill is in the process of being restored.

A good detour at this point is to visit a Cistercian convent roughly half an hour's drive away from Les Borges, and reached via Arbeca and Belianes: the 12th-century Cistercian **Monastery of Santa Maria del Vallbona** (Tuesday to Sunday 10.30am–1.30pm and 4.30–6.30pm, open Mondays in August). It is still run today by Cistercian nuns. The magnificent abbey church contains the remains of several former abbesses and also of Queen Violant of Hungary, who died in 1251. The convent also has a small museum and a library.

From Les Borges Blanques it's another 23km (14 miles) to **Lleida** (see page 68).

79

Tombs of the kings of Aragón

Olive groves, Les Borges Blanques

Barcelona

Route 13

The Ebro Valley

Amposta – Tortosa – Gandesa – Lleida (153km/98 miles) *See map on page 76*

This one-day-long romantic trip up the Ebro Valley should definitely be included in any beach holiday in Catalonia. The idyllic landscape – and Tortosa itself – also bears several scars from the fierce fighting between the Republicans and Franco's troops during the Civil War.

Tortosa (pop. 31,000), 19km (11 miles) away from Amposta, is the industrial and economic centre of the Ebro Valley area. It is picturesquely situated on the Riu Ebre. Three bridges connect the new part of the town in the west with the older part in the east. The first people to settle the hill above the town, where the fortress of La Suda can be seen today, were the Iberians. After Roman occupation, the town remained in Moorish hands for some 300 years (9th century onwards), until it fell to Count Berenguer IV of Barcelona in 1148. Tortosa suffered at the hands of Philip V (1707) and also Napoleon's troops at the beginning of the 19th century, but it was almost completely destroyed in 1936, during the Spanish Civil War.

On the Carrer de la Ciutat lies Tortosa's impressive **Cathedral**, built on the ruins of a former mosque. Construction work on it began in 1347 and lasted until well into the 15th century. The main facade is baroque in origin (18th-century), while the bell-tower has an admixture of Moorish elements. Inside the cathedral, the Capella Mare de Déu de la Cinta is particularly worthy of note. The baroque chapel (the second on the right) contains part of the belt of the Virgin Mary. The double ambulatory with its Flamboyant decoration is also very fine, as is the 14th-century Gothic altarpiece behind the high altar, depicting *Christ on the Mount of Olives*. The 13th-century Romanesque cloister with its wooden vault can only be reached from outside the church, via the Puerta de la Olivera (1705) on the Plaça de la Cinta.

Leave the cathedral and cross over to the **Palau Episcopal** opposite. This 14th-century Gothic building has a very fine inner courtyard surrounded by Gothic arcades. Just a few yards from the episcopal palace is the Palau Oliver de Boteller, with its 15th-century facade.

The Carrer Sant Domènec contains a wonderfully harmonious Renaissance ensemble: the Collegi de Sant Luis (founded by Charles V in 1544), with its Plateresque architecture reflecting the transition from Gothic to Renaissance (in the inner courtyard, the first of the three rows

Baroque detail, Tortosa Cathedral

Palau Episcopal, inner courtyard, and a veteran of the times

of arcades contains medallions depicting the kings of Aragón), and nearby the long buildings forming part of the 16th-century monastery of Sant Domènec. The monastery church contains the municipal museum (Monday to Friday 9am–3pm). The fortress above the town is the Castell de la Suda; it was originally built by the Moors and later became the residence of King Jaume I. Today it has been converted into a state-run hotel *(parador)*, and there is a magnificent view of Tortosa and the Ebro Valley from the top.

The view from the fortress

As far as trips in the vicinity are concerned, to the west of Tortosa is the ★ **Serra dels Ports de Beseit** mountain range, with its highest peak, Mont Caro (1,447m/ 4,745ft). A trip into the unexpectedly bizarre mountain landscape around Els Requers and Alfara de Carles (24km/15 miles) is also ideal for hikers and nature lovers.

The route continues through the Ebro Valley now, via Aldover and Xerta and along the C-12 and C-43 to **Gandesa** (pop. 3,400), which is situated at the centre of an important wine and olive producing area. The town lies picturesquely at the foot of the Puig Cavaller (962m/3,150ft). It was founded by the Moors, and the 13th-century church of De la Asunción is actually built on the ruins of a mosque. There are several fine Gothic buildings in the middle of the town, including the 14th-century town hall. The impressive buildings of the Gandesa Agricultural Cooperative date from 1919; the art nouveau halls at the winery were designed by César Martinell.

The Ebro Valley

One very good detour from Gandesa is to travel to **Miravet**, 23km (14 miles) to the east. The village is dominated by the former castle of the Knights Templar. The outlying potters' quarter is justly famous. Although it now draws tourist coaches, the family potteries still work traditionally, mixing their own clay and following shapes which go back to Moorish times.

The castle at Miravet

Some 5km (3 miles) beyond Gandesa on the C-12B is a village whose name recalls a dark chapter in Catalonian history. **Corbera d'Ebre** was almost completely destroyed by Franco's troops. The ruins of this village and its church have been left as a silent witness to the destructive power of war.

The next stop on the C-12B is **Ascó**, famous mainly for its enormous atomic power station which is cooled by the Ebro. The reservoir at Flix has a massive hydroelectric dam. A ferry trip is necessary to get from one side of Flix to the other.

From here it is another 58km (36 miles) across agricultural land irrigated by canals to reach the provincial capital of Lleida (see page 68).

Art History

Opposite: cloister column detail, La Seu d'Urgell

The first important cultural traces were left in Catalonia by the Greeks. They founded Emporion *(see page 41)* in around 600BC. Later the Romans left their mark on much of the region. They mostly settled the area around Barcelona and Tarragona. Visigothic structures (mostly churches) are few and far between, as are Moorish ones.

Romanesque

Romanesque portal, Salardú

It was the Romanesque style (ca 950–1200) which was the first to leave really impressive architecture right across the region. The end of the first millennium AD saw a period of political stability in Catalonia, which was starting to become independent and develop its own regional pride. The counts of Barcelona financed enormous monasteries and churches for the Benedictine Order, and these became important cultural centres (e.g. Ripoll, *see page 58*).

The Early Romanesque parish churches had one nave and a maximum of three apses. After the so-called Roman liturgy was introduced in around 1050, many of these churches were extended and given an extra transept and apse so that the altars necessary for the new form of liturgy could be properly accommodated.

Calvary in St Joan

83

Master architects and gifted sculptors from Southern France and Lombardy worked on many churches in Catalonia, especially in the Pyrenees, and gave these narrow-towered buildings their special identity (e.g. Vall de Boí, *see page 66*). It was local masters, however, who painted the magnificent frescoes in the apses of these Catalonian village churches; the main motif shows Christ as *Pantocrator*, ie ruler of the world. Many of these frescoes have been lost over the years as the churches have fallen into disrepair, but quite a number have been transferred to museums. The Museu Nacional d'Art de Catalunya (MNAC; *see page 23)* contains the finest and largest collection of apsidal frescoes in Spain and along with the Museu Diocesà in Vic *(see page 71)* also contains the best collection of Gothic art in Catalonia.

Gothic

Monestir Santes Creus, cloister

During the Gothic period (1150–1450) Catalonia achieved its heyday of economic prosperity. The secular nobility and the townspeople left several impressive buildings, especially in the fast-developing cities, that testified to their political and economic power. Fine examples in Barcelona are the Barri Gòtic *(see page 20)*, the old royal shipyard (Els Reials Drassanes) and the Exchange (La Llotja).

The Catalan and Aragonese kings sponsored the construction of several Cistercian monasteries in Southern Catalonia. Pointed arches, ribbed vaults, rose windows and stained-glass windows were the new architectural features. Inside the churches, altarpieces – often illustrating the lives of saints – were among the most magnificent items during this period.

The Renaixença

In contrast to the glory of the Gothic period, the Renaissance, baroque and neoclassical eras left hardly any traces in Catalonia. The region was too involved in conflicts between Spanish kings and in defending its own political autonomy. It was only during the 19th century that it finally began to recover economically and also artistically. Catalonia experienced a *renaixença*, or rebirth, in its language, its literature and above all in its architecture.

From 1860 onwards, plans for a generously laid-out section of Barcelona called the Eixample were drawn up by Ildefons Cerdà. His ideas, considered quite revolutionary at the time (leafy inner courtyards, height regulations, social housing), also provided a platform for younger architects to put their theories into practice.

Modernisme

Casa Batlló in Barcelona

Modernisme is the Catalan version of art nouveau, and flourished between 1880 and 1925. It began in Barcelona, on the site of the razed citadel where the first world fair was held in 1888. It was here that Barcelona's young architects first had the opportunity to present their revolutionary ideas. They combined new building techniques (concrete and iron construction) with neo-Gothic ideas and forms borrowed from nature. Using natural materials such as wood, ceramics and glass, they created highly individual structures that reflected the light, the climate and colour of the Mediterranean. This originality on the outside was extended to interiors: architects designed special furniture, doors and lamps to go with their creations.

The best known exponent of *Modernisme* was Antoni Gaudí (1852–1926). Stylistically the most revolutionary of the architects, he worked almost entirely in or near Barcelona. His work is infused with a deep mysticism and sense of unity, and he devoted the final third of his life to just one building, the church of the Sagrada Família *(see page 24)*. During its construction he became increasingly pious, and even secluded himself on its site. He was killed by a tram on his way to vespers at the age of 75.

Sagrada Família

Luis Domènech i Montaner (1850–1923), not only an architect but also a university professor and politician, had a far stricter attitude towards *Modernisme* than Gaudí. His buildings are based on strict geometrical forms, but gain a flexibility from their decoration, which often features unusual materials. Many Catalans consider him, rather than Gaudí, to be the leading exponent of *Modernisme*.

Josep Puig i Cadafalch (1867–1957) can really be defined as the 'thinker' among the Modernist architects. A professor of history and a politician, his work is more oriented towards Northern European influences. Unlike Gaudí, who seemed almost possessed, Puig i Cadafalch abandoned his Modernist view of art after World War II in favour of a neoclassical one.

Literature

There was some excellent prose being written in Catalan as far back as the Late Middle Ages. The first document ever to be written in the language, the *Homilies*, dates from the 12th century. Famous later authors include Ramon Llull (13th century), Arnau de Vilanova (14th century) and Joanot Martorell (15th century). The poet Jacint Verdaguer (1845–1902), the dramatist Angel Guimerà and the novelist Joan Maragall all epitomised the renaissance of secular Catalan literature. They were followed by writers such as Josep Pla (1897–1981) from Palafrugell, or Mercé Rodoreda (1909–83). Two leading lights of contemporary Catalan literature are Juan Marsé (born 1933) and Manuel Vázquez Montalbán (born 1939); their novels and detective stories are often set in the *demi-monde* of Barcelona's Old Town.

85

Painting and Sculpture

'Let us consider what it means to be a native of the Mediterranean. It means that we are equidistant from the bright light of the Tropics and from the almost ghostly darkness of the North. The Catalans have a natural ability to see the unity in things, and in the way those things relate to one another. The sea and the special Mediterranean light create this magnificent clarity.' This statement of Antoni Gaudí applies in particular to such Catalonian artists as Barcelona native Joan Miró (1893–1983), Salvador Dalí (born in Figueres, 1904–1989) and Pablo Picasso (1881–1973). Picasso, the only one of the three not to have been born in Catalonia, spent his youth and early academic years in Barcelona before leaving for France in 1904. Miró also worked in Paris, but always retained close ties with Barcelona, where he played an important role in the opening of a remarkable museum on the Montjuïc. Of the three, Dalí *(see page 39)* was the keenest on his Catalonian homeland, where he died.

Joan Miró
Dalí Museum in Figueres

These three personalities aside, Catalonia's artistic potential completely stagnated during the Franco regime, and only reappeared in the 1980s. The abstract and futuristic work of artist Antoni Tàpies, the architectural trend known as *Nou Urbanisme* and Barcelona's Europe-wide importance as a centre of design all document this recent artistic renaissance.

Festivals and Folklore

Catalonia has developed several of its own rituals and dances over the centuries, some of which can be quite a surprise. One such is the *castell*, or 'human pyramid', which can often be as high as 10m/32ft. The strongest men in the group form a circle, the next group climbs on their shoulders, and so on. At the very top of the pyramid is a young boy known as the *enxaneta* (literally: weathervane). If he manages to retain his balance and stand up for longer than three seconds, the *castell* is considered successful.

The ritual known as the *correfoc* – groups running at night through the streets on public holidays wearing strange-looking animal masks, with devilish faces – dates back to the legend of St George and the dragon. The groups appear at local *festas* making a great deal of noise and may fling firecrackers around indiscriminately. When the devil turns up everyone has to take cover.

Most towns have their own *gegants*, papier-mâché figures, often 3m/10ft high, representing various famous people or typical characters from the particular locality. They are manipulated by young men who only have a small peephole at the front of the colossus to help them get their bearings as they dance.

Dancing and the Sardana

Dancing and music are also a very important part of Catalonian tradition. Sentimental seafaring songs known as *havaneras* originated in the former Spanish colony of Cuba and today they are heard mostly in the Costa Brava resort of Calella de Palafrugell. Rings of dancers seen in market squares on Sundays are performing the *sardana*, which is open to everyone. The *sardana* is thought to be 500 years old and of uncertain origin. The dancers form

Dancing the Sardana

a circle (men always stand to the left of the women), hold hands and execute a series of short *(pasos curts)* and long *(pasos llargs)* steps forward, sideways and backwards. The dancers have to count the steps under their breath, and this gave rise to a joke throughout the rest of Spain about Catalonians being 'so calculating that they even count while they dance!'

The dancing groups *(rotllanes)* are accompanied by an unusual 10-man orchestra, the *cobla*. To the rhythm (usually 6/8) of the double bass and a small hip-drum, nasal melodies are played by a small flute *(flabiol)*, a kind of oboe *(tenora)* and other wind instruments. Forbidden during Franco's time, the *sardana* has long been a symbol of Catalan solidarity – of 'sticking together, come what may'. These days anyone is welcome to join in, and they can do so in the cathedral square in Barcelona (Saturday 6.30pm, Sunday 12 noon).

Festivals in Barcelona

The festival of Sant Jordi (St George) is celebrated on **23 April** in honour of Catalonia's dragon-killing patron saint. Flowers and books are on sale everywhere.

On around **15 August**, there is the Festa Major de Gràcia; music and street decorations in the district of Gràcia.

On **24 September** all Barcelona relaxes in honour of patron saint La Mercè: *castells* appear in front of the Town Hall and giant statues are paraded through the streets.

Festivals elsewhere in Catalonia

Pre-Lent **Carnival** is celebrated in many towns, especially Sitges, where colourful floats are showpieces for gays in gorgeous drag.

Holy Week processions take place in many towns, such as Girona, when Roman legionaries march through the streets. In Verges there is an an extraordinary ancient Dance of Death, with skeletal fingures wielding scythes.

Roman legionaries in Verges

The festival of La Patum in Berga, held at **Corpus Christi**, is entirely different; its highlight is a fire-breathing dragon and a re-enactment of the battle between the Moors and the Christians.

St John's Eve, **June 23**, is important throughout Catalonia, when fires are lit, fireworks let off – there is a display in Barcelona, on Montjuïc – and runners carrying torches come down from Mount Conigó.

In the middle of **July** water processions take place in many coastal towns to honour the Verge del Carmen.

Between **24 and 28 July** there's an enormous firework festival in the town of Blanes.

Tarragona goes crazy on **23 September** during its annual fiesta in honour of St Thekla, and the alleys in the Old Town should definitely be visited at this time.

87

Food and Drink

Cuisine

There are two main types of Catalan cuisine: rather substantial home cooking (sausages, beans, venison, olive oil), and a broad variety of seafood dishes. When the Catalan fleet started conquering other lands in the 13th century, Catalan cuisine was subjected to new influences, especially from Italy. The first ever Catalan cookbook, *Llibre de Coch*, was written in 1490 by Rupert de Nola, chief cook of King Ferdinand of Naples, the son of Alfonso V of Aragón. Italy gave Catalonia its noodle dishes; rice *(arròs)* has only occupied a regular place in Catalan cooking since the 19th century, however. The world-famous *paella*, a rice dish available in several variations, comes from the Valencia region. French cooking arrived only very late on the scene, during the 19th century. Several vegetarian and wholefood restaurants have sprung up in recent years, but one still gets the impression that it's hard for the Catalans to change their eating habits. These involve a steady daily intake of small hors d'oeuvres known as *tapas* (mostly seafood with high-calorie sauces, mussels, mushrooms and omelettes in all kinds of variations) in the bar round the corner, followed by an enormous family meal in the evening.

Porrones are part of the drinking culture

89

Sauces play a major role in Catalan cuisine. One very popular accompaniment, especially to grilled food, is the mayonnaise-like sauce known as *allioli* which is usually served cold, and consists of chopped garlic, olive oil and egg yolk. *Romesco*, a red sauce consisting of olive oil, garlic, crushed paprika and almonds, is served either warm or cold with grilled food and salads. *Picada* is a paste made of ground garlic, parsley, almonds, hazelnuts and toasted bread. The most famous warm sauce is *sofregit*: olive oil, onions, garlic and tomatoes are steamed and usually served as a side-dish for fried food.

Hors d'oeuvres in Catalonia can be light but also very substantial. Salads come in several variations: *esqeixada* is garnished with fish, *amanida catalana* contains sausage and ham, and *xató* contains sardines or tuna. A popular starter in the Pyrenees is *mongetes amb botifarra* – sausages served on beans cooked in pork dripping.

Tempting seafood

As far as main courses are concerned, the seafood ones are recommended the most: *graellada de mariscos*, for instance, an assortment of fish and crustaceans, or the fish stew known as *suquet de peix*. Shrimp dishes are served either *a la planxa* (fried) or *a la marinera* (steamed and garnished with *allioli* or *romesco*). The best meat dishes include *conill* (rabbit) which is served with all kinds of side-dishes including *cargols* (snails), and *pollastre* (chicken), which can also be found in the amazing dish

A variety of pastries

llagosta amb pollastre, consisting of prawns, chicken – and chocolate sauce! Those keener on rather less adventurous fare should opt for the delicious meat stew known as *escudella de pagès*.

Pudding in Catalonia is generally sweet. *Crema catalana* is a pudding made of eggs, milk and caramelised sugar. *Menjar blanc* consists of honey, almonds and milk. There are some fine variations with regard to cheese, too: *serrat* is a sheep's cheese from the Pyrenees, and *tupí* is the same thing sprinkled with brandy. Most low-priced restaurants serve yoghurt or fruit after the main meal, however.

Drinks

Home-grown wines

90

Beer *(cervesa)* is popular in Catalonia, but the main beverage is still wine, which is grown locally in large quantities. There are eight official wine regions; here is a selection. One very good red table wine is *Priorato* from the Tarragona region, which also produces good whites such as *Falset*. The rosé known as *Trepat* is grown near Penedès, and *Garnatxa* is a delicious dessert wine from the Costa Brava. The house wine *(vi de casa)* in restaurants generally tends to be good, too. The sparkling wine known as *cava* from the region around Sant Sadurní d'Anoia is now world-famous; it's at its best dry *(Brut* or *Brut nature)*. Coffee can be enjoyed in various ways: as a black espresso *(café sol)*, with a drop of milk *(tallat)*, with lots of milk *(amb llet)*, diluted with water *(café americano)*, or laced with rum *(cremat)*.

Sparkling speciality

Cava – the Catalan Answer to Champagne

Just 50km (30 miles) away from Barcelona is Catalonia's 'sparkling wine capital', Sant Sadurní d'Anoia *(see page 26)*. In the mid-19th century it was still a sleepy little village, but things altered dramatically when vineyard owner Josep Raventós i Domènech travelled to France and paid a visit to Dom Perignon in the Champagne region. Deeply impressed by the *méthode champenoise* practised there he began producing his own sparkling wine back in Catalonia, calling it *cava* rather than champagne because of the copyright problem. Catalonian sparkling wine has gained an international reputation, and Sant Sadurní d'Anoia has long since become busier than it once was. A visit to Can Codorniu, the Raventós family home commissioned from leading art nouveau architect Puig i Cadafalch by Josep's son Manuel, is still an experience.

By the way, the nearby wine region of Vilafranca del Penedès, home of all the delicious wines with the *penedès* mark of origin, definitely deserves a visit. There's also an interesting Wine Museum *(Museu del Vi)*. Spanish wine is fun to aim – try drinking it out of *porrons*, the traditional long-necked glass or leather vessels.

Restaurants

Lunch in Catalonia is eaten comparatively late, between 2pm and 5pm, and supper between 9pm and midnight. Remember that many restaurants are closed on Sunday and/or Monday, and that reservations in advance are usually a good idea. Most restaurants in Catalonia have a *menu del día*, or menu of the day; consisting of three courses plus a beverage, it is the cheapest way of dining out.

The following suggestions for Catalonia's main centres are listed according to three categories: €€€ = expensive, €€ = moderate, € = inexpensive.

Medieval atmosphere in a parador

Barcelona
€€€Set Portes, Passeig Isabel II 14, tel: 93 319 3033. Once the haunt of Dalí, Miró and García Lorca, this restaurant remains a bastion of first-class Catalan cuisine. **€€Senyor Parellada**, c/Argentería 36, tel: 93 310 5094. Local dishes in a colourful, lively ambiance in the Gothic quarter of Santa María del Mar. **€€Can Culleretes**, Carrer Quintana 5, tel: 93 317 6485. The oldest restaurant in the city dates from 1786. **€€Los Caracoles**, Escudellers 14, tel: 93 302 3185. The best known of the many restaurants occupying the side streets of the Rambla. Rustic decor, often busy.

Girona
€€€Albereda, Albereda 7, tel: 972 226002. One of the best restaurants in the city. **€L'Hostalet del Call**, C. Claveria. Rustic restaurant with traditional food.

Tarragona
€El Tiberi, (Carrer d'en Martí d'Ardenya 5, tel: 977 235403. Catalan buffet-style restaurant. **€€Eugeni i Montse**, Plaça de la Font 10, tel: 977 221 068. Serves specialities of the region, including Paella Marinesa. **€Mediterraneo**. A lively café, especially in the evenings. Seafront terrace.

On the coast
€€€Carles Camós Big-Rock, Barri de Fenals, Mas Nou, Platja d'Aro, tel: 972 818012. Great country cooking in an old mansion. **€€Can Salvi**, Passeig del Mar 23, Sant Feliu de Guixols, tel: 972 821337. A traditional restaurant with excellent fish. **€€Bahia**, Passeig del Mar 19, Tossa de Mar, tel: 972 340322. Local speciality: *cim-i-tomba*, a fish stew.

Inland
€€€Sa Punta, Platja de Pals, tel: 972 667376. Speciality is a delicious lobster salad. **€€La Borda de Betrèn**, C. Mayor Betrèn, in front of the church, Vielha, tel: 973 640032. Hearty food from the Val d'Aran. **€€La Cabana d'en Geli**, C. de Sant Llorenç 35, Solsona, tel: 973 482957. Try the prawns with artichokes.

Pyrenean restaurant

Aigües Tortes national park

Active Holidays

People are growing increasingly keen on keeping fit and in good shape during their holidays, rather than just lying around on the beach. Catalonia provides limitless possibilities in this respect, and also has just the kind of varied landscape to cater for all tastes. Those keen on peace and quiet can go fishing or hiking; the more adventurous can go river-rafting, jump into deep snow from helicopters – or bungee-jump off several extremely high bridges.

Diving on the Costa Brava

Sailing and water sports

Catalonia's coast is its number one attraction, and its calm waters and mild climate make it a paradise for water sports enthusiasts. Windsurfers tend to head for the northern part of the Costa Brava, where the *garbí*, a southeasterly wind, will fill the sail even though the waves stay reasonably small. Water-skiing and waterscooters are of course available at all the main resorts, and at the Platja d'Aro there's parascending for the more adventurous. Divers and snorkellers will find much of interest along the rockier parts of the Costa Brava, as well as in the diving grounds of the Illes Medes near L'Estartit. Children will love the *Aquatic parcs* along the coast; the one in Roses is called 'Aquabrava', and the one in Lloret del Mar is 'Water World'. For more information contact the Associació de Parcs Aquàtics, Provença 106, Barcelona, tel: 93 419 5648.

For yachting, there are around 40 harbours, the smallest in Portbou and the largest in Santa Margarida. The latest harbour, Barcelona's Port Olímpic, is worth a trip in its own right. These aren't the most peaceful places, however. For more information, contact the Associació Catalana de Ports Esportius i Turístics, Balmes 156, Barcelona, tel: 93 415 3301, fax: 93 415 4426.

Golf

Spanish golfers, e.g. Severiano Ballesteros, have a good reputation – and the greens in Catalonia are excellent. Golf's been played here since 1914, and there are more than 30 courses to choose from. For further information, contact the Federació Catalana de Golf, Aribau 282, 08006 Barcelona, tel: 93 414 5262, fax: 93 414 5672.

Skiing

The Pyrenees are a real paradise for skiers. The traditional area at La Molina, or the region around Baqueira-Beret are both excellently equipped, but Catalonia has 18 winter sports centres in all and the cross-country skiing routes and pistes are highly attractive everywhere (the Val de Núria has 98 pistes alone). For more information, and also the latest weather and snow reports, contact the Associació Catalana d'Estacions d'Esquí i Activitats de Muntanya, Camps i Fabres 3–11, 08006 Barcelona, tel: 93 416 0194, fax: 93 415 2983, snow report tel: 93 416 0194.

Angling

The streams and lakes of the Pyrenees are a fishermen's paradise. Angling permits may generally be obtained from the regional tourist authorities. For further information, contact the Federació Catalana de Pesca, c/Lluça 9, Barcelona, tel: 93 330 4818.

Hiking

Catalonia has 3,000km (1,860 miles) of hiking routes, and the brochure 'Catalonia on Foot', available from all tourist offices, describes most of the 100 or so coastal and mountain routes. The GR 92 path between Portbou and Blanes (which follows the E10 European long distance footpath) is particularly beautiful. Further information may be obtained either from the Federació d'Entitats Excursionistes de Catalunya or from the Senders de Catalunya, both on Rambla 41, 08002 Barcelona, tel: 93 412 0777.

Hiking routes are well signed

River-rafting

The region around the Noguera river has become an important centre for white-water rafting, canoeing and kayaking. Starting-points for trips are Sort and Rialp *(see Route 9, page 64)*, and information can be obtained from local tourist offices.

Kayaks for competition in La Seu d'Urgell

Mountain biking

The foothills of the Pyrenees are a paradise for mountain bikers eager to keep fit. Further information on everything to do with cycling can be obtained from the Federació Catalana de Ciclisme, C. Fontanella 11, 08010 Barcelona, tel: 93 301 2444.

Getting There

Opposite: look out for local steam trains

By air

There are three international airports in Catalonia. El Prat de Llobregat in Barcelona is 15km (9 miles) from the city centre. Trains between the airport and Sants station leave every half hour and take 20 minutes. Buses leave every 15 minutes from Pl. de Catalunya and Sants and take 30 minutes.

Girona-Costa Brava is increasingly busy, Reus-Costada Daurada less so and are charter-only airports which do not operate in winter. Both have fly/drive facilities. An airport at La Seu d'Urgell near Andorra handles domestic flights.

Iberia, the Spanish airline, is the principal operator in Barcelona and offers regular money-saving deals on flights and fly/drive.

In the UK: Iberia House, 10 Hammersmith Broadway, London W6 7AL, tel: 0845 601 2854.
In the US: 6100 Blue Lagoon Drive, 33126 Miami, tel: 800 772 4642.

By car

The Spanish border is about 13 hours from the channel ports by motorway, 10 hours from Paris. But anyone arriving by car with time on their hands would be well advised to take the French *routes nationales* rather than the toll motorway – the roads are very well-surfaced, the landscape is often more attractive, and the decision saves quite a lot of money.

The winding coast road (the N-114 in France, becoming the N-260 in Spain) crosses the border at Portbou. The N-9 national road from Perpignan crosses at Le Pertus and becomes the N-11. Beside it the A-9 motorway becomes the A-7 as it reaches the La Jonquera border point – both are busy in summer and though the motorway queues can be longer, they tend to move faster.

By rail

The Paris–Barcelona line comes over the border at Portbou, and it takes about 11½ hours from Paris Austerlitz to Barcelona's Sants station. Trains stop at Girona, but it is necessary to change at Sants and take a Valencia bound train to go further down the coast to Tarragona.

By bus

Regular bus services run from most large European cities. Eurolines' services from London's Victoria Coach Station (tel: 0990 808080 or 0207-730 3466) go to Barcelona, stopping at Figueres and Girona, a journey of 24 hours.

Catalonia by road

Easy parking in the country

Getting Around

By car

In between the motorways and national highways, Catalonia is criss-crossed by a network of regional and local roads, mainly going north–south, following the rivers coming down from the Pyrenees and making hard work of east–west journeys. Some of the roads more than compensate, by scenery or lack of traffic, for what they may lack in smoothness.

C for Catalunya

The maximum speed limit in built-up areas is 60kmph/37mph), on country roads 90kmph/55mph, trunk roads 100kmph/62mph and motorways 120kmph/74mph. Seat belts are compulsory outside built-up areas. It's best to drive cautiously, because the fines in Spain can be very high. In the cities, and in Barcelona especially, parking spaces are few and far between. Never park in the opposite direction to the traffic, or on stretches of pavement marked with yellow paint: the car is almost certain to be towed away within a few minutes. The multi-storey car parks are expensive, but safer.

Motorists should bring along their licence, car registration papers and insurance documents. All cars should display a nationality sticker; headlight beam converters and a replacement bulb kit are also compulsory. A bail bond in case of accident is advisable but not compulsory.

Car hire

To hire a car you must be at least 18 and have a valid licence (an international licence is not essential). Charges are usually calculated at a daily rate, plus mileage and insurance, and are comparable with charges elsewhere in Europe.

Breakdown

The police will take care of things in towns or cities and in the country. For emergency assistance, tel: 092.

By rail

Travelling by train in Catalonia with RENFE, Spain's national train network (and also on suburban trains in the Barcelona region, run by Ferrocarrils de la Generalitat) is very simple and also quite cheap. There are various categories of trains. The Tranvía is a local train, which stops at all, or most stations. An Expresso or Rapido is long-distance, stopping only at main stations. The Talgo, Ter and Tren Estrella are luxury trains, first and second-class.

By bus

Most towns in Catalonia can be reached by bus, and fares are inexpensive.

Facts for the Visitor

Plan of medieval Pals

Travel documents

For stays not exceeding three months, citizens of the European Community, the US, Canada and Australia need bring only their passports. A residence permit has to be applied for where longer stays are involved.

Customs

Since the abolition of the duty-free system within the European Union, if you are an EU visitor you may buy as much as you like during your journey, provided it is for your own use. If you bring back more than the following guidance levels for consumer goods, customs may ask you to show the goods are for your own use: 800 cigarettes, 200 cigars, 1kg of tobacco, 90 litres of wine, 10 litres of spirit and 100 litres of beer per person.

'Duty-frees' are still available to travellers to and from countries outside the EU.

Tourist information

In the UK: Tourist Information Office of Spain, 22–23 Manchester Square, London W1U 3PX, tel: 020 7486 8077.
In the US: Tourist Office of Spain, 666 Fifth Avenue, New York NY 10103, tel: 212-265 8822, fax: 212-265 8864; 8383 Wilshire Boulevard, Suite 960, Beverley Hills, CA 90211, tel: 213-658 7188, fax: 213-658 1061.

In Catalonia: Tourist information of Barcelona, Catalonia and the rest of Spain, Paseo de Grácia, 105, Barcelona, tel: 93 238 4000 (from outside Catalonia) tel: 012 (in Catalonia); Oficina de Turismo, Rambla de la Llibertat, 1, 17004 Girona, tel: 972 226575; Patronat de Turisme, Fortuny, 4 , 43001 Tarragona, tel: 977 233415.

Exchange regulations

There is no limit on the number of euros that can be brought into the country, nor on the amount of foreign currency (though very large sums should be declared).

Currency

In February 2002, the euro (EUR) became the official currency used in Spain, along with most other member states of the European Union. Euro notes are denominated in 5, 10, 20, 50, 100 and 500 euros; coins in 1 and 2 euros and 1, 2, 5, 10, 20 and 50 cents.

With most credit and cash cards, you can obtain money 24 hours a day at many cashpoint machines.

Opening times

Souvenir fans

Banks: Monday to Friday 9am–2pm; in summer 8.30am–1.30pm, Saturday until 1pm.

Shops: Usually 9am–1pm and 4.30–7pm. Department stores are open 10am–8pm. Shopkeepers in the resorts stay open during lunchtime and also late into the evening.

Museums: Apart from the odd exception, closed all day on Monday, on Sunday afternoons and on public holidays.

Government departments: Monday to Friday 8am–3pm.

Post offices (Correus): weekdays 9am–2pm.

Restaurants: Very often closed on Sunday evening and Monday.

Public holidays

New Year's Day; 6 January (Epiphany); Good Friday; Easter Monday; 1 May (Labour Day); 24 June (Midsummer's Eve); 15 August (Assumption of the Virgin); 11 September (Catalonian National Day); 12 October (Discovery of America); 1 November (All Saints' Day); 6 December (Spanish Constitution Day); 8 December (Immaculate Conception); 25/26 December (Christmas).

Post

As well as post offices, stamps *(sellos)* can be bought from *estancos* (tobacconists) and hotel reception desks. Post abroad can take from four days to a fortnight. Always send important mail registered – the postal *express* system is fast and reliable.

Telephoning

In all the main tourist centres there are telephone offices where you pay after the call. International calls are cheaper between 10pm and 8am, as well as on Sunday; local calls are cheaper after 5pm and cheaper still after 11pm.

International calls may also be made from public telephones *(internacional)* using coins, but phone cards

Modern phones take cards

(tarjetas de telefónica), available from all tobacconists and post offices, are more practical.

First dial 00, wait for the tone, then dial the rest of the code for the country you want (for the UK dial 00-44; US and Canada dial 00-1), followed by the local code (omitting any initial zero) and then the number itself. A beep announces the end of the call.

Tipping
Even where prices are inclusive it is usual to tip waiters and taxi drivers an extra 5–10 percent. Porters, hairdressers and chambermaids should be given at least €1–2; tour guides and bus drivers on excursions, €2–3. With taxi drivers, round up the sum to the next euro. Porters at the airport have fixed rates..

Voltage
Usually 220 volts AC; sometimes still 120-125 volts AC. Adaptors can be bought at all major airports.

Health
Since 1998 EU nationals are entitled to emergency medical treatment. Treatment is paid for on the spot, but the money is reimbursed when you get back home. However, it is still strongly advised to take a E111 form (obtainable fom post offices in the UK) in case of hospitalisation.

For accidents…

Chemists are helpful with minor complaints. Called *farmàcies* or *farmacias*, they display green or red crosses. They should display notices giving details of a local emergency service; otherwise ask the police.

Town halls post surgery hours of clinics. The main towns have hospitals with 24-hour emergency departments. In Barcelona, the number to call in an emergency is 93 218 1800.

Crime
There's a relatively high risk of theft at the tourist centres along the Costa Brava and in Barcelona, so the following rules apply: never leave anything in your car, never carry more money on your person than you need, and leave your passport or identity card at your hotel. Be especially careful when getting money out of automatic tellers.

…and incidents

Emergencies
Emergency services, tel: 112, for police, fire brigade and ambulance.

Diplomatic representation
The nearest consulates are in Barcelona:
UK: Avinguda Diagonal 477, tel: 93 366 6200.
US: Paseo Reina Elisenda 23, tel: 93 280 2227.

99

Accommodation fit for a count

Accommodation

Information about hotels and other accommodation (addresses, prices and categories) is available from the Spanish Tourist Board and local offices. The comprehensive hotel register *(Guía de Hoteles)*, published annually, can also be obtained from booksellers for around €10.

Accommodation in Spain can be subdivided into the following categories: hotels *(hoteles, 1–5 star)*, apartment houses run on a hotel basis *(hoteles-apartamentos, 1–4 star)*, hostels which resemble inns *(hostales, 1–3 star)* and guest houses *(pensiones, 1–3 star)*. While the guest houses usually only offer rooms with full board, the establishments in the other categories can be *residencias*. State-run accommodation comes in the form of *paradores nacionales*, hotels in places that are either very scenic or very out-of-the-way. Often housed inside old castles and palaces, the *paradores* are usually luxurious, and their restaurants serve quality local food.

The following suggestions for some of the most popular spots are listed according to three price categories: **€€€** = expensive; **€€** = moderate; **€** = inexpensive.

Aiguablava
€€€Aigua Blava Hotel, Platja de Fornells, tel: 972 622058, fax: 972 622112. Family-run 4-star hotel, perhaps the best on the entire Costa Brava.

Andorra la Vella (country code 376)
€€€Novotel Andorra, Prat de la Creu, tel: 873603, fax: 873653. Contains tennis courts, fitness room and gym.**€€Cerqueda Hotel**, Mossèn Lluis Pujol 20, tel: 722235, fax: 722909. Good hotel with open air pool.

Arties
€€€Parador Don Gaspar de Portolá, Ctra de Baqueira, tel: 973 640801, fax: 973 641001. Housed in the impressive 16th-century castle of the Portolá family, whose ancestor, Don Gaspar, conquered California.

Barcelona
€€€Ritz, Gran Via 668, tel: 93 318 5200, fax: 93 318 0148. A venerable hotel with the highest international standards. **€€€Balmes**, Mallorca 216, tel: 93 451 1914, fax: 93 451 0049. Nice location in Eixample, excellent breakfast buffet. **€€€Colón**, Av. Catedral 7, tel: 93 301 1404, fax: 93 317 2915. In the Gothic Quarter, opposite the cathedral. Individually furnished rooms. **€€Majestic**, Passeig de Gràcia 70, tel: 93 488 1717, fax: 93 488 1880. Classy and tasteful. **€€Oriente**, Rambla 45, tel: 93 302 2558, fax: 93 412 3819. A little run down, but with history, having been here since 1930. **€Cortés**, Santa Anna 25, tel: 93 317 9212, fax: 93 412 6608. Quiet location off the Rambla.

Hotel Majestic

The Oriente

Blanes
€€Pí-Mar, S'Abanell 8, tel: 972 352817, fax: 972 335062.

Cadaqués
€€Playa Sol, Platja Pianc 3, tel; 972 258100, fax: 972 258054, This fine hotel includes tennis courts and swimming pool among its facilities. **€€Port Lligat**, Av. Salvador Dalí, s/n, tel: 972 258162, fax: 972 258643. A peaceful location on the sea in Dalí's fishing village.

Calella de Palafrugell
€€Sant Roc, Pl. Atlàntic 2, tel: 972 614250, fax: 972 614068. Superb view of the coast from the terrace.

Cambrils
€€Port Eugeni, Rambla Jaume I, 49, tel: 977 365261, fax: 977 365613. Situated at the harbour, with swimming pool.

Cardona
€€€Parador Duques de Cardona, tel: 93 869 1275, fax: 93 869 1636. Hill-top old castle with beautiful views.

Espot
€€Roya, Sant Maurici 1, tel: 973 624040, fax: 973 624144. Family owned for 100 years. Arranges apartments for visitors to the Aigüestortes national park.

Girona
€€Costabella, Av. de Franca, 61, tel: 972 202524, fax: 972 202203. Within easy walking distance of the Old Town.

There are a number of places to stay in the Old Town, including the delightful **€Hostal Bellmirall**, Bellmirall 3, tel: 972 204009 (only 7 rooms, so book in advance).

L'Escala
€€Nieves Mar, Passeig Maritim 8, tel: 972 770300, fax: 972 773605. A comfortable hotel with swimming pool and tennis courts.

L'Estartit
€€Panorama, Av. de Grecia 5, tel: 972 751092, fax 972 750119. The largest hotel in town, with 154 beds. **€€ Bell Aire**, Església 39, tel: 972 751302, fax: 972 751958. Modern, comfortable hotel not far from the beach.

Two-star night

La Seu d'Urgell
€€Parador de La Seu d'Urgell, Santo Domènec 6, tel: 973 352000, fax: 973 352309. Comfortable hotel with swimming pool, by the cathedral. **€Andria**, Passeig Joan Brudieu 24, tel: 973 350300, fax: 973 351425. Pension with a friendly atmosphere in a modern building.

Parador de La Seu d'Urgell

Lleida
€€€Condes de Urgell, Av. de Barcelona 17–27, tel: 973 202300, fax: 973 202404. Situated on the road out to Barcelona. Although this high-rise hotel is not very attractive from the outside, it offers guests every comfort. **€Principal**, Pl. Pahería 7, tel: 973 230800, fax: 973 230803. In an old town alley, near the town hall.

Palamós
€€Trias, Passeig del Mar, tel: 972 601800, fax: 972 601819. Long-established, elegant seaside hotel.

Puigcerdà
€Del Lago, Av. Dr. Piguillem 7, tel: 972 881000, fax: 972 141511. A small but very pleasant 13-room hotel with garden and swimming pool.

Roses
€€€Almadraba Park, on Platja Almadrava, tel: 972 256550, fax: 972 256750. Comfortable 4-star hotel in a quiet location. Restaurant with a good reputation.

Sant Carles de la Rápita
€€Aparthotel La Ràpita, Pl. Lluis Companys, tel: 977 741507, fax: 977 741954. A comfortable hotel. **€€Miami Park**, Av. Constitución 33, tel: 977 740351, fax: 977 742551. Has an excellent restaurant attached, the Miami Can Pons. Smaller hotels include the **€Llansola** and **€Juanito** on Playa Miami.

Sant Feliu de Guíxols
€€€**Eden Roc**, Punta de Port Salvi, s/n, tel: 972 320100, fax: 972 821705. Large hotel in beautiful grounds in the Port Salvi district. Also a number of €hotels and €pensions in the centre.

Sitges
€€€**San Sebastian Playa**, Port Alegre 53, tel: 93 894 8676, fax: 93 894 0430. A very comfortable and elegant hotel situated right on the beach of the same name.

Solsona
€€**Gran Sol**, on the road to Manresa, tel: 973 480975. Facilities include tennis courts and swimming pool.

Tarragona
€€€**Imperial Tarraco**, Rambla Vella 2, tel: 977 233040, fax: 977 216566. Rises above the town like a Roman palace, and has great views over the sea. €€**Lauria**, Rambla Nova 20, tel: 977 236712, fax: 977 236700. Housed in a palace with romantic courtyard. Quiet, despite being right on the Rambla Nova. €**Astari**, Via Augusta 95–97, tel 977 236900, fax: 977 236911. Good restaurant.

Tortosa
€€€**Parador de Tortosa**, tel: 977 444450. Elegant parador in the medieval castle, with views across the town and the River Ebro. Excellent restaurant.

Tossa de Mar
€€€**Gran Reymar**, Platja Mar Menuda, tel: 972 340312, fax: 972 341504. Beautifully located, with a view of the bay. Mar Menuda beach just below is good for swimming.

Tremp
€€€**Segle XX**, Pl. de la Creu 8, tel: 973 650000, fax: 973 652612. The best hotel in town, good for an overnight stop.

Val de Boí
Hotels and hostels in the villages include: €**Hostal Fondevila** in Boí, tel: 973 696011, with modern rooms, and €**Pensió L'Aut** in Errill la Vall, tel: 973 696048, opposite the church and built in the vernacular style.

Valls
€€**Hotel Félix**, Ctra. Tarragonera, km17, tel: 977 609090, fax: 977 605007.

Vielha (Val d'Aran)
€€€**Tuca**, Ctra. Salardú, tel: 973 640700, fax: 973 640754. Mountain hotel, open all year round and with its own lift.

Palms and pools await

Index